CICADA MADNESS

Timing, Fishing Techniques, and Patterns for
Cracking the Code of Epic Cicada Emergences

Dave Zielinski

STACKPOLE BOOKS

Essex, Connecticut
Blue Ridge Summit, Pennsylvania

STACKPOLE BOOKS

An imprint of Globe Pequot, the trade division of
The Rowman & Littlefield Publishing Group, Inc.
4501 Forbes Blvd., Ste. 200
Lanham, MD 20706
www.rowman.com

Distributed by NATIONAL BOOK NETWORK

British Library Cataloguing in Publication Information available

Library of Congress Cataloging-in-Publication Data

Names: Zielinski, Dave, 1974– author.
Title: Cicada madness : timing, fishing techniques, and patterns for cracking the code of epic cicada emergences / Dave Zielinski.
Other titles: Timing, fishing techniques, and patterns for cracking the code of epic cicada emergences
Description: Essex, Connecticut : Stackpole Books, [2023] | Includes bibliographical references and index. | Summary: "Both annual and periodical cicada hatches are feasts for fish across the country and a boon to the anglers out to catch them. This is the first book dedicated to the patterns, techniques, and science of locating the best hatches of these insects"— Provided by publisher.
Identifiers: LCCN 2023008666 (print) | LCCN 2023008667 (ebook) | ISBN 9780811771825 (paperback) | ISBN 9780811771832 (epub)
Subjects: LCSH: Bugs (Fishing lures)—United States. | Cicadas—Life cycles—United States. | Fly fishing—United States.
Classification: LCC SH448 .Z54 2023 (print) | LCC SH448 (ebook) | DDC 799.12/2—dc23/eng/20230317
LC record available at https://lccn.loc.gov/2023008666
LC ebook record available at https://lccn.loc.gov/2023008667

be around that fish could find and eat them. The year 2020 brought the COVID-19 pandemic but also Brood IX in parts of Virginia, West Virginia, and Maryland. In 2021 the "Great Eastern Brood" or Brood X, emerged from Indiana to Washington, DC, and was exploited with mass media attention coast to coast. Misinformation and hype were abundant on every platform: television, internet, social media, and print. Even fly shops located far outside the distribution of Brood X advertised plans for "the bugs to come" and sold stickers, T-shirts, and an assortment of imitations for the event that would never arrive in their local waterways. With the same research, scouting, and pre-trip planning, we were able to fish this emergence in one primary Pennsylvania location, with little reason to break the old rule: "Never leave rising fish to find rising fish!"

Having the ability to fish periodical cicadas three years in a row has validated how we approach the impending emergences and accelerated the knowledge we were able to gain about the insect, environmental factors, and fish behaviors. This book is the culmination of the notes and experiences with these and many other emergences. We have applied the same techniques when understanding subsequent emergences, to a high degree of success. The same fishing tactics apply regarding annual cicadas, which are also included here. I have compiled our thoughts and observations, and included the insights of others who have shared their experiences chasing cicadas and the fish that eat them.

The author with a junior-size carp during a periodical cicada emergence

The occurrence of the annual cicada became of interest, too, as they occur each year, mid- to late summer in the East, but earlier in the West. Fish of all kinds will target the insects when they are available. In the late-summer months, eastern bass and carp will eat off the surface throughout the heat of the day. Much like chasing hopper or cricket plagues—those years when the expected numbers of grasshoppers, crickets, and ants in western states are at near-biblical numbers—we started to find the predictable and fishable cicadas each year in famous, prolifically written about trout rivers and lakes, like the Green River in Utah and the Colorado River at Lees Ferry, as well as seldom talked about or secret waters that will remain nameless to shield them from increased pressure and spot burning, all too common in the social media age. You will be surprised at how many locations across the United States harbor fishable occurrences of these wild and freaky insects.

Through this book, it is my desire to share my experiences fishing this unique and incredible insect emergence. My intent is to enable the angler to understand this unique insect in simple terms, how to find them, time the emergence, and scout waterways to have a successful fishing experience. I have included an extensive library of patterns to imitate the periodical and annual varieties of cicada from my own proven designs, local patterns, dependable guide flies, and commercially available flies. I hope to introduce you to an experience that you will not soon forget, and that you can use these tactics to identify, locate, and fish patterns of the cicadas that occur wherever you may fish.

The Cicada: A Brief and Slightly Scientific Overview for the Fly Angler

THE PHONE RANG THREE TIMES BEFORE I HEARD "HEY DUDE" ON THE other end of the line. "It's starting!" I responded with little control of the excitement in my voice. Following weeks of preparation, scouting, and wandering the local woods and waterways, I had just found the first of millions—perhaps billions!—of Brood VIII *Magicicada* at my local lake. *Magicicada*, otherwise known as the three species of 17-year periodical cicadas, was scheduled to emerge in 2019 where I reside in southwestern Pennsylvania. For us, as fly anglers, this meant the long-awaited return of fishing that can only be described with a single word: *epic*. Through building an understanding of the natural world and the insect itself, and our passion for fly fishing, we have created a unique and coveted experience we look forward to each year that periodical cicadas occur.

A dry-fly angler's year usually starts with aquatic-born insects like midges, caddisflies, stoneflies, and mayflies. Warm days in March bring Blue-Winged Olive hatches, followed by various caddis in April. As the warmer temperatures of May approach, it all breaks

The first of millions

loose with the prolific hatches. Caddisflies, Hendricksons, Sulphers, Green Drakes, and a host of other mayfly, caddisfly, and stone-fly species emerge and provide excellent fishing opportunities. By the time June starts, the major hatches are waning in the East, and terrestrial season is just getting started. Here in the East, we are prepping our boxes for our western migrations to Montana, Colorado, Utah, Wyoming, and Idaho to extend our dry-fly season in the Rockies. In the West, June and July brings the end of snowmelt and runoff, and the beginning of big stonefly hatches leading to mayflies. The season unfolds fast, with fish beginning to hide on the edges of undercut banks as soon as the grass grows. Enter the terrestrial. Both fish and fly anglers are no strangers to terrestrial insects. Trout have always risen to the unlucky ant, hopper, or cricket that inadvertently found its unfortu-nate way into the water. Fly-fishing authors have written volumes about the importance

Periodical cicada with its wings expanded. All cicadas have two pairs of wings. MIKE ENGELHARDT

of terrestrials in a trout's diet since the beginning of fly fishing in America. Ed Shenk, Dave Whitlock, Vince Marinaro, and a host of others gave us the foundation of terrestrial fly patterns covering ants, beetles, and hoppers. But despite the varieties and availability of the insects, cicadas have been absent in the majority of fly-fishing literature. Could it be so good that it is purposely kept secret?

As summer forges on, it is an opportunistic time for the fish, keen on eating a variety of food sources, big and small. In certain years, they will see more terrestrial insects than in others. Grasshopper "plagues" are a 1-in-10-year occurrence in many areas of the West, and while a curse to farming and agriculture, the angler can bet on this as a prime event for fantastic hopper fishing. "Mormon Crickets," the large shell-backed crickets found across the West, made an appearance by the millions in July 2022 in Utah, not seen since 12 years earlier. In cicada years—whether it is the prolific periodical varieties found in the Midwest and East or a localized bumper crop of annual species found just about everywhere—the entire ecosystem will experience more bugs than can be imag-ined. Birds, reptiles, amphibians, and mammals large and small will feed heavily on the available biomass that many will experience only once in their lifetime. Of course, where there is water, there will be fish taking the opportunity to feed on the protein source, too.

Cicadas are among the largest group of insects, with over 3,000 identified species worldwide. They are part of the family Cicadidae of the insect order Hemiptera. Insects in this order are considered "true bugs," which includes aphids, ladybugs, beetles, and hoppers in addition to cicadas. Hemiptera is derived from the Greek words *hemi* and *pterus* which means "half-wing," of which the cicada has a pair of half-length secondary wings. Bugs in this order are characterized by having mouthparts that enable them to feed on fluids extracted from plants and roots. This looks like a long straw that protrudes from

A *Magicicada septendecula* periodical cicada. The periodical species are easily identified by their red eyes and primarily orange-and-black coloration as adults.

A typical annual variety found in the eastern and southern United States, *Neotibicen*

the beak, or mouthparts, of the cicada. This piece of anatomy exists in all phases of the insect's life.

Inclusive to the Cicadidae family are both annual and periodical varieties. Annual cicadas occur each year roughly between May and September in varying numbers, much like grasshoppers or beetles. These annual varieties make up the vast majority of species found globally. "Periodical" describes the unique, synchronized emergence of a small subset of species based on the cadence of their life cycle. There are only seven periodical species, but they have the longest life cycle of any insect in North America, emerging on a predictable cycle of 13 or 17 years, occurring in May or June of their anticipated year. Periodical cicadas are of particular interest, as they only inhabit the landmass contained in the eastern half of the United States. There are no other periodical species known to exist anywhere else in the world.

As adults, the noisy, creepy, big-eyed cicadas are among the largest of terrestrial flying adult insects, followed by their grasshopper, locust, and beetle cousins. To a non-angler, the sight of an enormous insect with bulging eyes is enough to reproduce "the Wilhelm Scream." To a fly angler, the words "large terrestrial" will raise eyebrows, perk ears, and silence any other conversation to enable some innocent eavesdropping. The experienced old-timer in the room might even peer over their newspaper and reading glasses to do a cred check and listen in. Cicadas are enormous insects by any standard; some species can exceed 2 inches in length. Compare this with the tiny and weightless early season Blue-Winged Olive mayfly tied on a tiny size 20 hook and 6X tippet and imagine the size of hook and tippet you'll need for a 2-inch fly. Yep, that big.

Both annual and periodical varieties have a similar life cycle, behaviors, and appearance. As immature insects, they live underground and feed on plant roots, and are of little interest to fish or anglers. As adults, they finish their life's purpose to make a bunch of noise, mate, lay eggs, and set the next generation into motion. Both periodicals and annuals can occur in prolific numbers and use unique evolved tactics for evading predators, mating, and proliferation. We will discuss periodical cicadas and contrast the species, identification, and behaviors of the annual variety in parallel. Both occur in fishable numbers and are worthy of the time spent understanding, locating, and fishing their occurrences.

THE PERIODICAL CICADA—*MAGICICADA*

The term "periodical cicada" defines the seven species of the genus *Magicicada* uniquely occurring in the eastern half of the United States. For a species to be "periodical," it must have a fixed development time and appear in a location on a regular interval. For periodical cicada species, this interval is a 13-year or 17-year *synchronized* emergence cycle. Synchronization, as you will see later, is the key to the species success in mating and survival.

There are three species of 17-year cicadas: *Magicicada septendecula*, *M. septendecim*, and *M. cassini*, and four species of 13-year cicadas: *Magicicada trecendecula*, *M. neotredecim*, *M. tredecim*, and *M. tredecassini*. These species occur roughly as far west as Oklahoma, north and east to New York, and south through Louisiana. There are no other 13- or 17-year periodical cicadas anywhere else in the world.

A pair of Brood X periodical cicadas on a multiflora rose bush, June 2021

Identification of the adult form of the periodical cicada is generally easy. All species have a black to dark brown body with orange stripes and defining red eyes. Clear, glassy wings have thick, orange outer veins. A defining factor is the size of each species. All periodicals are inherently similar in coloration and behavior. Some annual species of the American West are similar enough to the periodical colors that some fly patterns in proper sizes can mimic both eastern and western bugs. Keep this in mind when imitating the various species in your locale. From the fish-eye view (looked at from below), these species share a common shape, so size is a key difference. Coloration of abdomens shows varying concentrations of black, brown, and orange. Keep this in mind when tying imitations. For instance, a black or brown body material with an orange rib mimics the darker, more black varieties, while an orange body material with a black or brown rib mimics the orange variety. It pays to have a mix of patterns that match both, as you will discover that the majority of emergences have populations of each species present. Specifically, general size and coloration guidelines are as follows:

Left to right: *M. cassini, M. septendecula,* and *M. septendecim* varieties. DAN MOZGAI, WWW. CICADAMANIA.COM

SPECIES	SIZE	COLORATION
Magicicada septendecim, M. tredecim, M. neotredecim	30–35 mm	Abdomen more orange than black or brown. Described as orange with black stripes or "mostly orange with black or brown."
Magicicada septendecula, M. trecendecula	20–25 mm	Abdomen more black than orange. Described as black with orange stripes or "mostly black with orange."
Magicicada cassini, M. tredecassini	22–27 mm	Abdomen almost all solid black with very little to no orange on segmentations.

Broods

In 1893, entomologist Charles Lester Marlatt with the US Department of Agriculture proposed the classification of "Broods" for periodical cicadas, utilizing Roman numerals to differentiate them. Numerals I to XVII are reserved for 17-year cicadas, and numerals XVIII to XXX for 13-year cicadas. The year 1893 started the system with Brood I, 1894 with Brood II, and so on for 17-year cicadas. For 13-year cicadas, the numbering also started in 1893 with Brood XVIII. This allocated for one brood per year for all 13- and 17-year possibilities. Later research has led to the identification of only 15 broods, not 30; however, the naming system remains in use today. Individual broods are made up of populations that emerge in the same year in a geographical location. I like the way Dr. Gene Kritsky describes them: "Think of broods as a 'class reunion.'" The species are the same insect; however, the "age class" and period between the various brood emergences is different. In most cases, a brood will contain multiple species of cicadas that occur at a certain time and place. These broods fit together like pieces of a puzzle when looked at

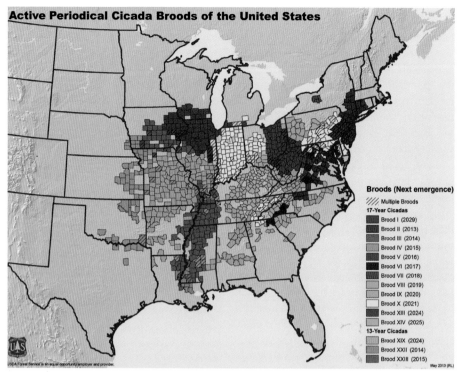

Photograph of USFS brood distribution map: "Active Periodical Cicada Broods of the United States," Andrew M. Liebhold, Michael J. Bohne, and Rebecca L. Lilja, USDA Forest Service Northern Research Station and Northeastern Area State & Private Forestry. PUBLIC DOMAIN

geographically. Note that 13-year cicadas dominate the central or westernmost states in range, and the 17-year are dominant in the eastern, northern, and southern states. Each emergence of 17-year cicadas contains all three species, and each emergence of 13-year cicadas contains all four species in most cases, with exceptions of Broods VI, VII, XIII, and XXII (see Table 1.1). Overall, there are 12 broods of 17-year cicadas and 3 broods of 13-year cicadas, rarely overlapping in time and geographic areas. Because of this, it is almost possible to encounter periodical cicadas "most years, somewhere"—if you do the homework, math, and scouting and don't mind driving or travel. Broods are as small as the very geographically isolated Brood VII, found in a small part of upstate New York, to as large as Brood XIX, the "Great Southern Brood," which contains the largest geographical area inhabited by the insect. While predictable in occurrence, the evolution of broods is somewhat of a mystery best explained by genetic mutations and science. The table below identifies the broods, species, and general geographic distribution of the 13- and 17-year cicadas.

TABLE 1.1: PERIODICAL CICADA BROOD DISTRIBUTION

BROOD (CYCLE)	LAST OCCURRENCE	NEXT EMERGENCE	SPECIES	LOCATIONS (STATES)	NOTES OF INTEREST
I (17)	2012	2029	M. septendecim, M. septendecula, M. cassini	Tennessee, Virginia, West Virginia	Named the "Shenandoah Valley Brood." Heavy emergence in the valley and along the Blue Ridge Parkway.
II (17)	2013	2030	M. septendecim, M. septendecula, M. cassini	Connecticut, New York, New Jersey, Pennsylvania, Maryland, Virginia, North Carolina, Georgia, Oklahoma	East of the Appalachian Mountains and along the eastern seaboard. Odd, disjunct populations exist in Georgia and Oklahoma.
III (17)	2014	2031	M. septendecim, M. septendecula, M. cassini	Missouri, Illinois, Iowa	Named the "Iowan Brood." Northwestern Illinois to central Iowa contain areas of heavy emergence.
IV (17)	2015	2032	M. septendecim, M. septendecula, M. cassini	Missouri, Iowa, Kansas, Nebraska, Oklahoma, Texas	Named the "Kansan Brood," this is the farthest western broods of periodical cicadas.
V (17)	2016	2033	M. septendecim, M. septendecula, M. cassini	SW Pennsylvania, Ohio, West Virginia, NW Maryland, NW Virginia	One of the only broods that borders a great lake, Lake Erie, almost entirely on Ohio's lakeshore to as far south as Virginia. The very southwest corner of Pennsylvania has prolific emergence along the Youghiogheny River. Believed to be extinct on Long Island, New York.
VI (17)	2017	2034	M. septendecim, M. septendecula	Western North Carolina, NW South Carolina, NE Georgia	Brood VI inhabits range shared with other broods, often confusing scientists on the actual range. Confirmed core brood exists around the Pisgah National Forest.
VII (17)	2018	2035	M. septendecim	New York	Named the "Onondaga Brood." Only found in a small area in Upstate New York near Syracuse, west of the finger lakes.
VIII (17)	2019	2036	M. septendecim, M. septendecula, M. cassini	Pennsylvania, Ohio, West Virginia, Oklahoma	Smaller in distribution, yet prolific where it occurs. East of Pittsburgh to Johnstown, Pennsylvania, and west to the Ohio and West Virginia border.
IX (17)	2020	2037	M. septendecim, M. septendecula, M. cassini	West Virginia, Virginia, North Carolina	This brood is isolated in pockets where it is found, typically in higher elevations. This is a bit of a curse to the angler as the rivers and lakes in these states sit in the deep valleys created by the Appalachian Mountains. There may be large amounts of insects on the mountaintops, and little to none in the deep valleys.

TABLE 1.1: PERIODICAL CICADA BROOD DISTRIBUTION

BROOD (CYCLE)	LAST OCCURRENCE	NEXT EMERGENCE	SPECIES	LOCATIONS (STATES)	NOTES OF INTEREST
X (17)	2021	2038	*M. septendecim, M. septendecula, M. cassini*	New York, Pennsylvania, Delaware, New Jersey, West Virginia, Virginia, Maryland, North Carolina, Tennessee, Georgia, Ohio, Indiana, Illinois, Kentucky, Michigan	Named the "Great Eastern Brood." Second largest in distribution. Southern Ohio and Indiana are areas of prolific emergence as well as south-central Pennsylvania to Washington, DC. This brood has very close overlap with Brood XIV, and often stragglers are identified.
XIII (17)	2007	2024	*M. septendecim, M. cassini*	Michigan, Wisconsin, Indiana, Illinois, Iowa	Historically found throughout Michigan, these are thought to have gone extinct there; currently appear densely from Chicago to Springfield, Illinois.
XIV (17)	2008	2025	*M. septendecim, M. septendecula, M. cassini*	New York, New Jersey, Pennsylvania, Ohio, Maryland, Massachusetts, Tennessee, Virginia, West Virginia, Kentucky, Indiana, Georgia	Two distinct groups: the first from north Georgia to central Ohio, the second in central Pennsylvania. Extremely prolific and dense in these areas. Often confused with Brood X because of overlapping boundaries.
XIX (13)	2011	2024	*M. tredecim, M. neotredecim, M. tredecassini, M. tredecula*	Alabama, Arkansas, Georgia, Illinois, Iowa, Kansas, Kentucky, Louisiana, Missouri, Mississippi, Maryland, North Carolina, Oklahoma, Tennessee, South Carolina, Virginia	Named the "Great Southern Brood." Two distinct bands: central to southern Illinois, Kansas, and Indiana; and along the coastal plain from Alabama, Georgia, North Carolina, and Virginia. Prolific in both areas.
XXII (13)	2014	2027	*M. tredecim, M. tredecassini, M. tredecula*	Ohio, Kentucky, Mississippi, Louisiana	Named the "Lower Mississippian Brood." Extremely small, isolated brood near Baton Rouge, Louisiana, and a disjunct population near the Ohio-Kentucky border.
XXIII (13)	2015	2028	*M. tredecim, M. neotredecim, M. tredecassini, M. tredecula*	Indiana, Illinois, Arkansas, Mississippi, Missouri, Kentucky, Tennessee, Louisiana	Named the "Mississippi Valley Brood." Occurs from south of St. Louis to southern Louisiana along the Mississippi Valley.

Evolution of *Magicicada* Species

To give you an idea how long these insects have been around, let's look at the evolution of periodical cicadas. Scientists know little as to why and where they originated, but we do have evidence that the evolution of 13- and 17-year cicadas has been impacted by climate change and ice sheet and glacial movements over billions of years. Scientists have confirmed through genetic testing that all seven species of *Magicicada* evolved from a single common ancestor about 3.9 million years ago. It is believed that the 13-year -*decim* species were created about 3.9 million years ago from a species comprising both -*decula* and -*cassini* DNA. This parent species diverged again about a million years later into the separate -*decula* and -*cassini*. It is believed that the modern 13-year species are the result of 17-year *septendecim* hybridized with a 13-year *tredecim* to create a 13-year *neotredicm* species, the seventh species of *Magicicada* we know today. Initially however, there were not both 13- and 17-year species.

Why 13 and 17 years? There are no definitive answers on the long life cycle or the evolution of periodicity of cicadas; theories on underground immature nymphal development, life-cycle-lengthening evolutions, and predator satiation are continually being understood today.

The Mysteries of Periodical Cicada: Periodicity, Prime Numbers, Predator Satiation, and Brood Separation

There is significant fascination with the mysteries of the periodical cicada. Some of this has to do with being some of the oldest evolved species of insects known today. The longer a species exists, the more evolutionary adaptations occur, strengthening those that enable proliferation and eliminating those that don't. Because of this, theories are abundant, and comparisons to other species try to explain what we don't understand. Some of the more interesting theories provide us as anglers insight into the when, where, and why associated with an emergence.

Periodicity refers to "occurring at regular intervals." Protoperiodicity is recurring but irregularly, which is a condition common with annual species of cicadas, where species may be prolific in some years and scarce but not entirely absent in others. It is unclear if periodical cicadas evolved from protoperiodicity through dominant genetics, environmental catastrophes, feeding habits, predator satiation, fixed developmental cycle, or life cycle lengthening (A. Martin and C. Simon, Temporal Variation in Insect Life Cycles: Lessons From Periodical Cicadas, *BioScience* 40[5] [1990]: 359–67). There are continued and ongoing studies on truly protoperiodical annual cicadas to better understand and validate the theories on the 13- and 17-year life cycles of *Magicicada* species. The common denominator seems to be time—millions of years to evolve to what we know today. Understand that periodical cicadas are much more predictable—allowing you to prepare for an emergence—they absolutely will happen in their year of emergence. With annual varieties that follow protoperiodicity, it is much harder to predict the prolific years where their numbers make a significant difference in the fishing.

A prime number is one that is only divisible by one and itself. It is quite peculiar that periodical cicada emergence cycles are prime numbers. Again, this evolution to a prime number—13 and 17 years depending on the species—is among the longest life cycle between birth and mating of any animal. This spaces the peaks so far apart that all predators are unlikely to peak on the same cadence. The sheer numbers of insects that emerge overwhelm the entire environment.

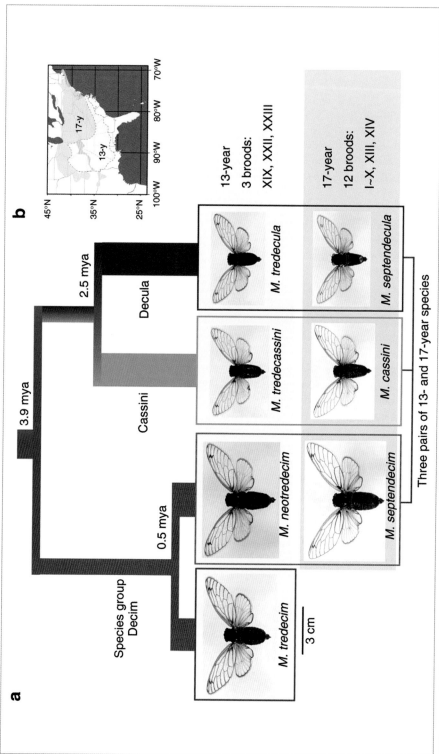

Triplicate parallel life cycle divergence despite gene flow in periodical cicadas. *Commun Biol* 1:26 (2018). IMAGE COURTESY OF T. FUJISAWA ET AL.

How many cicadas do you see? Freshly emerged periodical cicadas from the night before, just a few feet from the stream. Epic numbers of insects ensure proliferation of the species through "predator satiation." June 2016, southwest Pennsylvania.

They can't get them all. An unlucky periodical cicada stuck in a spiderweb. Brood V, 2016.

"Predator satiation" is an adaptive tactic used to evade predation by overwhelming numbers. Basically, there's so many at once that predators can't possibly eat them all. Periodical cicadas emerge in epic proportions; the first to emerge are often eaten, but the predators cannot keep up and are "satiated" over time. This ensures that the species can proliferate through a massive availability to the environment. There's simply "plenty to go around" for everybody—this includes being eaten!

On the predator side of the conversation, predator cycles increase and decrease at a much shorter rate, unlikely to coincide with an emergence. Most predators of cicadas— birds and mammals—have a much shorter life span than the periodical cicada. It is highly unlikely that a predator or group of predators can eat enough of the insects to prohibit successful mating. For example, if a predator cycle has an upswing every six years, it will peak the 1st, 6th, 12th, 18th, and so on. This lessens the chance of overlap with a periodical cicada emergence. It is believed that the evolution to true periodicity and a lengthening life cycle enabled cicadas to synchronize emergence at intervals spaced far apart (13 and 17 years), directly to evade peaks in predation. Most predators live shorter life spans, which makes it hard to adapt, evolve, and teach their young and adapt to cicada cycles, as multiple predator generations occur within the cicada's 13- and 17-year cycles.

Common predators of adult cicadas are birds, including robins, red-winged blackbirds, starlings, and other woodland birds that inhabit the high canopies of forests. On the ground, snakes, turtles, and squirrels have been observed to focus attention on finding and eating cicadas. George Daniel shared an experience in central Pennsylvania where he witnessed a mother black bear and her cubs targeting cicadas on tree limbs over a period of several days on his way to fishing. Underground, where the cicada spends the majority of its life, the primary predators are not well understood; however, it's believed to be moles and voles. It's obvious that below the ground, any predation that occurs does not have any significant impact on cicada populations.

When periodical cicadas do occur, the ecosystem receives a huge boost in biomass, often having noticeable impacts. The Pennsylvania Game Commission in recent years published on its website a direct correlation in young turkey survival during the years a periodical cicada emergence occurred in an area. Wild turkeys mate and lay eggs in the spring, and by the time the summer solstice rolls around, juvenile turkeys are growing fast and foraging woodlots and fields, primarily eating insects under the watchful eyes of their mothers. The timing of periodical cicada emergences in May and June fit the wild turkey's life cycle like a glove. It is certain that other foragers of cicadas have similar upticks in numbers following cicada availability. But they can't catch them all!

Regarding interbreeding of broods, separation not only geographically but through 13- and 17-year emergence cycles prevents cross-breeding. Even though these are the same species of the insect, recall that they are a different "age class," defined by their brood emergence year. The first number that 13 and 17 have in common is 221. This means that every 221 years, a 13-year and a 17-year periodical emergence will overlap. The next time this overlap will occur is with Brood XIII (17-year brood) and Brood XIX (13-year brood) in 2024. The location of this clash will be near central Illinois. Scientists I have spoken to are preparing for this event—it is a once-in-a-lifetime chance to witness interbreeding between broods. As an angler I urge you to take note of this as well, if only for alternative motives, as it is sure to provide unbelievable fishing opportunities. A single brood produces unfathomable amounts of insects. Two coinciding broods emerging on the same schedule ought to produce a new definition of "epic proportion." No human alive today will experience this again, which continues to perpetuate some of the mystery surrounding cicadas. Because of the duration of time that passes between emergences, they can even evade scientists and research.

It becomes very hard to study a population of insects that only occurs decades apart. Contrast this with a typical aquatic insect like the *Baetis*, or Blue-Winged Olive. These can have up to four complete life cycles in a single year. You could effectively study several life cycles in a year of the insect. If you think of the typical career length of a scientist entering the workforce at 25 years of age, retiring at 65, that is 40 years of research opportunity. For an insect that occurs every 13 or 17 years, it is quite possible that the average scientist could study two or three emergences of a single brood. If you look into research of cicadas at the scientific level, you will see compilations of observation, research, and experiments that span the careers of many scientists picking up where others have left off. I have found this to be true for cicada research more than for any other insect.

General Life Cycle

Both periodical and annual cicadas begin their lives as eggs that hatch into nymphs several weeks after being deposited by their mothers on a tree branch. They will fall to the ground and immediately disperse, finding their way into the earth at the base of a tree. The growing cicada goes through several "instars," or nymphal stages of postembryonic development. Dr. Gene Kritsky, dean of Sciences at Mount St. Joseph University in Cincinnati, Ohio, and renowned author and cicada researcher, has determined through experimentation that the nymphal cicada will spend most of its life within a square meter of where it was

Newly hatched cicada larvae in a tree branch. CHAZZ HESSELEIN, ALABAMA COOPERATIVE EXTENSION SYSTEM, BUGWOOD.ORG

born. Once on the ground, the nymphal cicada will navigate to cracks in the earth and immediately seek fine roots of trees, grasses, and plants, then use its beak to pierce the root and suck xylem. Xylem is a transport tissue in plants that enables water and amino acids to be drawn from the ground upward into plant stems. Contrary to popular belief, the piercing of roots to access xylem does not harm the roots. Cicadas possess an enzyme that allows the puncture to heal itself and continue growth. The cicada will slowly move around a tree's root system, feeding on larger roots and molting as it grows to adulthood. It will remain deep in the soil, to be immune from temperature fluctuations and light.

The immature insect will molt several times throughout its underground life, at different rates. This molting process, common to all arthropods, is called "ecdysis," or the process of shedding the skin in order to physically grow larger. There are several theories that the signal for molting, which affects growth rate, is sensed by the cicada through changes in seasonal xylem flows during feeding. We don't know how the insect "counts" years, but seasonal xylem flows do present a change that is typical on an annual occurrence. There is also the possibility that periodical cicadas possess some sort of internal timing mechanism yet undiscovered.

Developmentally, the immature cicada goes through five instars, which scientists don't fully understand. Marlatt dug up 17-year cicada nymphs at various stages, finding variable data suggesting that the first instar lasted a year, the second instar two years, the third instar three or four years, and the fourth instar six to eight years. The fifth instar is the final stage of development into adulthood. The fifth instar nymph will be emerge from the soil in its final year of life and morph into the winged adult cicada. It was later discovered that 13-year cicada nymphs reach the fifth instar faster than 17-year cicadas, suggesting that either 13- or 17-year species develop slower or possess a dominant gene directly affecting development rate. (R. T. Cox and C. E. Carlton, Evidence of Genetic Dominance of the 13-Year Life Cycle in Periodical Cicadas (Homoptera: Cicadidae: Magicicada spp.), *American Midland Naturalist* 125[1] [1991]: 63–74). Generally, the 13-year cicada is in its fifth and final instar by 9 years, and the 17-year by 13 years.

Stragglers and Shadow Broods

It is more than interesting that the difference between 13 and 17 is 4.

There are occurrences of "straggler" emergences early or late for both species; however, these are not typically full population emergences. I observed this in 2021 during the Brood X emergence. I identified Brood XIV cicadas four years early in areas where there shouldn't have been a Brood X emergence. This is a common occurrence for broods that overlap in geographical distribution; Broods X and XIV are known to closely share these boundaries. Straggler or "shadow broods" occurrences can occur in fishable numbers; however, the occurrences will be much more localized where they happen to occur. For 17-year species, the straggler years are four years early, and for 13-year species, it is typically one year late. Scientists believe this will almost always occur because of the four-year developmental gap between species. Recall that 17-year cicadas develop slower, but may accelerate due to unknown factors, spawning a range of theories, one of them overcrowding of underground cicada nymphs (M. Lloyd and J. White, Sympatry of Periodical Cicada Broods and the Hypothetical Four-Year Acceleration, *Evolution: International Journal of Organic Evolution*, 30 [Dec. 1, 1976]: 786–801). Mystery yet surrounds these "straggling" events, as Dr. Kritsy explains: It is unclear if these stragglers are the offspring of successfully reproducing parent stragglers in areas where they occur in greater numbers and have been witnessed in the same geographic areas. Modern technology, the power of the internet, and community data gathering is allowing us to understand these events better. More on this later. Bottom line, as an angler, be aware of your area and check for straggler events surrounding waterways four years prior to a 17-year emergence and one year after a 13-year emergence.

Dr. Kritsky explains that cicadas, through their feeding habits, can detect seasonal change based on the flow of sap. This can clue us in to how cicadas mature to adulthood and determine emergence. It has been observed that odd weather patterns, such as freak winter storms that give way to abrupt springlike conditions, can create a sap flow, confusing the cicada's growth and molting patterns, and causing some portion of those insects to emerge a year early. Typically, this is very localized, based on weather patterns and geography unlikely to affect an entire region. Just like the straggler populations, it is unlikely for the full distribution to emerge early, and early emergences usually succumb to predation.

The rest of the underground life of the cicada is rather boring, as they quietly and happily suck on tree roots, slowly growing to maturity, having growth spurts, and molting. Things get really interesting in the final chapter of their adult lives as their emergence year approaches.

Emergence

In the spring of their emergence year, cicadas will begin to work their way toward the surface soil to about 1 to 10 inches below the surface and wait for specific conditions to trigger mass emergence. During this time, some cicadas will begin to make test runs to the surface, where they leave behind telltale signs that emergence is impending. This time of year will be late spring, which is generally wet across the periodical cicada's range. Very often, "mud turrets" will be built a few inches above the surface, which have a ⅜- to ½-inch hole indicating where the cicada nymph peeked above the surface during wet weather.

They build this structure to stay above the soggy topsoil. In areas with good drainage and fairly dry earth, the area will be absent of turrets, but holes can be seen. The cicada will not fully emerge, but retreat back until the right conditions are present. For

Cicada tunnels toward the surface soil.
©ROY TROUTMAN/SBPSTUDIOS

Cicada pushing through the surface soil, showing a cross section of a "mud turret."
©ROY TROUTMAN/SBPSTUDIOS

periodical cicadas, the magic conditions are a temperature of 64 degrees F at a depth of eight inches below the surface. In the eastern half of the United States, the only place where periodical cicadas exist, this will be sometime between late April and late May, with southern states occurring earlier. When conditions permit, in the middle of the night, the bone-white cicada nymphs will begin to break through to the surface and start their slow crawl upward on the nearest vertical surface. Often this is the very tree they were born under. A warm spring rain can accelerate the rise of the ground temperature, triggering the emergence. As the cicadas exit their underground lair, they will leave behind individual holes in the ground. There will be hundreds, even thousands, of these holes, indicating that this location was a significant mating site years earlier. Look for these clues and conditions when scouting for the impending cicada emergence.

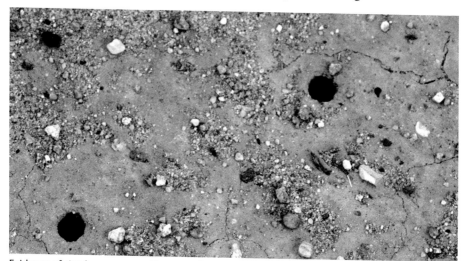

Evidence of cicada emergence. These are the holes left behind when the cicada leaves its underground life behind to begin its final form. WHITNEY CRANSHAW, COLORADO STATE UNIVERSITY, BUGWOOD.ORG

Cicada climbing tree trunk. ©ROY TROUTMAN/ SBPSTUDIOS

Cicadas emerging from their nymphal shuck. ©ROY TROUTMAN/SBPSTUDIOS

Nymphal shuck from a *Neotibicen canicularis*. Note the top is split open, at which point the adult emerges.

Newly emerged cicada. ©ROY TROUTMAN/SBPSTUDIOS

Partially morphed *Neotibicen linnei* found on the ground at the base of a tree. Normally, the emerging adult would be soft and white before it hardens and fully gains its adult colors. You can see that the back of the head and thorax is fully colored, indicating that the bug tried to fully morph but could not complete the process.

Adult cicada, fully morphed into a final stage adult, next to nymphal shuck. ©ROY TROUTMAN/ SBPSTUDIOS

Two cicadas on a tree branch.

Thousands of nymphal shucks fallen from a tree where a significant emergence took place over several days. Look for these signs when scouting for fishable numbers of bugs. ©ROY TROUTMAN/SBPSTUDIOS

Periodical cicada nymphal shucks left clinging to the tree where the adults emerged. Notice the partially morphed "stillborn" cicada. This cicada was weak or deformed and unable to fully emerge. ©ROY TROUTMAN/SBPSTUDIOS

Neotibicen linnei cicada shucks on an eastern redbud tree in August 2022. As you are walking near mature trees and streamside vegetation, look for the signs of emergence. It is likely that these were from the previous night or within the last two to three days. The adults are certainly nearby, likely congregating in the trees with the males singing, initiating the mating process.

Once the cicada nymph has crawled approximately 3 to 10 feet up a tree or other surface (street signs, telephone poles, nearby vegetation, buildings), it will begin its metamorphosis from nymph to flying adult, enabling it to complete its life's journey The nymphal cicada will begin to lose its outer white color and harden to a golden brown, at which point its nymphal shuck will split open at the thorax. Initially, the head and legs break free from the shuck, and the adult insect crawls away and pulls itself free. This exposes the wings, which are folded and curled, requiring fluid to inflate the vein structure to fully develop. At this point, the cicada is white with eerie red eyes—almost glowing for a short time as it hardens and fully transforms into a mature adult. The process takes from minutes to less than an hour depending on the air, humidity, and weather conditions. Once completely free from its nymphal shuck, the adult cicada will continue to reach full maturity, turning into the red-eyed, orange- and black-bodied, winged freak show we all love. The adult cicada will continue to climb higher into the trees, where it will remain for the next few days as its peers and prospective mates continue to emerge and build an army of unimaginable proportions. Left behind is the empty nymphal shuck, often still clinging to the tree as the adult moves on to the next phase in its life cycle. This will repeat each night for several days, with increasing numbers when the emergence is in full swing. In a few days, the nymphal shucks will fall from the trees, leaving behind several days' worth of empty shucks. In areas of high concentration, there will be several thousands. This is a key signal that peak numbers are approaching. In Pennsylvania where I live, I have found that during the lengthening daylight hours approaching the summer solstice is when peak numbers of bugs are aboveground and emergence of new adults has slowed drastically.

Temperature affects the adult cicada in two ways, the first of which is its mobility. All cicadas are diurnal. This means they are most active during the day. For the cicada, the

Female (top) and male (bottom) *Neotibicen linnei*. Note the two "pads" on the mid-section of the male. These are the tymbal covers.

hotter the better. It is a cold-blooded animal and dependent on an ambient temperature of at least 68 degrees F to become active. On cold, rainy days post emergence, the bugs will remain still, hiding on the underside of leaves or tucked into crevices of tree bark, waiting out the storm for brighter and sunnier days. We have experienced "low flying days" during fishable emergences on days that were cooler than normal or dark and rainy. The best time for active flyers seems to be the middle of the day, with a high sun and hot temperatures.

The second way temperature affects them is in their ability to attract a mate. All male cicadas, whether periodical or annual varieties, will use sound to attract mates. Only males are equipped with an ability to make sound. The males of all species of periodical cicadas possess tymbals—devices located on their sides that when flexed will make the noise that attracts females. Most male annual cicada varieties possess these, though there are species that do not. Crepitating cicadas, like the western *Platypedia* species, produce clicking or cracking sounds by flexing their wings and wing veins. Typically, the ambient temperature must also be at least 64 degrees F to enable the male cicada to make their love call. Much like "low flying days," cooler and wet-weather days will be absent of the cicada's love song.

On the hottest, brightest of days, the cicada calls occur in a grand chorus of thousands of individuals and can be in excess of 90 decibels, with some annual species exceeding 100 decibels. This is equivalent of standing next to a running lawnmower or a jackhammer! The sound of singing cicadas is a very important factor in locating cicadas in prolific and fishable numbers.

Mating Calls

The first five to eight days following the initial emergences, it will be quiet. The cicadas will be high in the treetops waiting, maturing, and preparing for the next phase of activity. The mating calls of the male suddenly begin with one bug, then two, then two million, increasing until a chorus is ever present during the daytime hours. The *-decim* species, the largest of the periodical cicadas—*Magicicada septendecim*, *M. tredecim*, and *M. neotredecim*—have a similar call, described in scientific literature as the "Pharoah" call. A male cicada makes a high- to low-pitched "Phaaa-roah." A full choir of male *-decim* cicadas sound like a sky full of rattlesnakes. The *-decula* species of cicadas—*Magicicada septendecula* and *M. tredecula*—make a fast-paced clicking noise, "tick, tick, tick," often in threes, that is followed by random short clicks and ticks. *Magicicada cassini* and *M. trecassini* also click rapidly followed by a higher-pitched "swheee" and descending-pitched "oohhhh." Scientists have identified various species and broods by the frequencies of their calls, and have determined that females only respond to the call of their own species as a way to inhibit crossbreeding. Regardless of the sounds of the male, when they are in a synchronized choir of song, it is unmistakable that cicadas are present.

In my experience, when these three species exist in an area, the *-decim* cicadas are overpowering; often you will hear them screaming at a great distance, like wavering AM radio static coming from the hillsides! This makes great background music when looking for willing fish eating the bugs. As anglers in the modern world, we all have videos on our smartphones of fish and fishing. When it comes to fishing, nothing makes my heart race more than reminiscing at my desk in the middle of winter while viewing a smartphone video with that sound in the background.

As the calls intensify over the next few days, the females are attracted to the sound; on hot days—the hottest, sunniest weather available—flying is at its best. Insects singing always leads to flying. This is an important factor in fishing during emergences. You may see signs of emergence, but until the singing occurs, there is no reason to fly. Remember that only the males sing to find mates. You may hear what sounds like a million bugs across the forest, but there's often at least twice that many when you include the silent females. If there is no flying, there are few chances for the bugs to inadvertently fall into the water where fish can find them. The females will fly from near and far to join the party. In turn, additional males will follow.

Be aware of other signs and signals in nature. Much like the saltwater striped bass or false albacore angler that watches for bird activity on the open ocean to locate schools of baitfish, pay attention to birds and odd behavior from ground mammals to locate areas of prolific bug activity. While having not experienced it myself, author and editor Geoff Mueller has told me to "look out for seagulls in the trees." There has been an observation of a connection between seagulls and heavy cicada activity on certain western tailwaters. Seagulls have identified the food source and target it like french fries in a fast-food parking lot!

A major difference between annual and periodical cicadas is their flying behavior and ability to evade capture. Periodicals are clumsy, poor flyers and easy to catch. Recall predator satiation—the sheer numbers of periodical cicadas is so immense it overwhelms predators so they cannot keep up. They do not need to be good flyers to proliferate the species. They are extremely easy to catch; you can walk up to any tree and simply pick them off. As anglers, this is to our great advantage. They are easily knocked down into the water and have no ability to extract themselves from the water's surface. We have seen cicadas "run out of gas" mid-flight and just plop to the surface of the water on their way to cross a stream or lake. Once in the water, it is over for that bug. Seldom, if ever, can a cicada recover itself from the water.

Annual cicadas on the other hand, fly with purpose. They are agile, aware, colored to match their environment, and can evade capture. Seldom can you spot one on a tree limb and get close enough to grab it by hand. I challenge you to first spot one in the canopy

Mating periodical cicadas. ©ROY TROUTMAN/SBPSTUDIOS

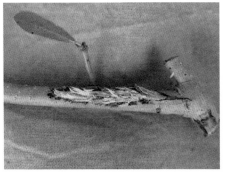

Ovipositing scars on a branch. CHAZZ HESSELEIN, ALABAMA COOPERATIVE EXTENSION SYSTEM, BUGWOOD.ORG

Neotibicen linnei. The female is on top. Note the sharply pointed end of her abdomen. The ovipositor is retracted, but just visible after the last segmentation. This will extend to slice into tree bark and deposit eggs.

"Flagging" on an oak tree, which is an indication of heavy egg-laying activity. ©ROY TROUTMAN/SBPSTUDIOS

and try to catch it barehanded. They have evolved to fly with skill to overcome predation. While photographing cicadas for this book, I was on a mission to catch several annual varieties, and it was a job to capture them! Some males of annual species will also emit a "sqwak" or "screech" sound when a bird or predator nears as a tactic to scare it. I have seen and heard *Neotibicen* species exhibit this behavior around my property in mid-August when eastern bluebirds would land in the fruit trees of my orchard. The birds would often flush and leave that tree. It seems to work!

For periodical cicadas, during the peak of the mating activity you will hear loud choruses of bugs, see flying activity, and find locations with millions, perhaps billions, of bugs concentrated in an area. Annual cicadas will be less densely concentrated, but the males' calls will be present. This area may be a single tree, a grove of hardwoods, or an entire forest. Where rivers and lakes border mature woods central to emergences, it is common for one bank to be full of activity and the other side to be completely absent of it. I have found that over the weeks of mating, these locations change. A productive area one week will become quiet, and the side of the river or lake that was once barren of activity will now be screaming. Luckily for anglers, the sound is easy to identify and will guide you to finding major congregations of cicadas.

Mating begins with a willing female attracted to a nearby singing male. She will flick her wings, indicating that she is ready to mate. Mating will commence, and the female will proceed to depositing her eggs. She will find a suitable tree, one that will carry her eggs and feed her young for future generations. Often this is a mature tree, with hardwoods seemingly a preference of periodicals. Desert annual varieties use box elder, alder, juniper, ponderosa pine, and scrub trees and shrubs; anything is fair game. It seems mating occurs in the highest of canopies, but ovipositing is often in the lower shrubbery for these species. The female possesses an ovipositor—a sawlike structure on her lower abdomen that enables her to cut into the spring growth terminal ends of branches and deposit her eggs. She will make several cuts and place 10 to 20 eggs in each slit. This will continue until all of her approximately 500 eggs are deposited. The cuts left behind will ooze tree sap and feed the hatching eggs as they grow into larvae. These cuts will heal; however, the scars can be seen in the following years.

The scars are a good sign for scouting potential sites for cicada activity in subsequent years. However, these scars are often high in a mature tree's canopy. Another sign left behind is known as "flagging." This is a result of the egg-laying female depositing her eggs in very young growth, leaf stems, and fine branches. This sometimes kills or stuns the branch, causing the leaves to wilt and die. This stands out in the summertime forest easily, especially on hardwood trees such as red and white oak, maple, and walnut. It is a dead giveaway—literally and figuratively—that cicada activity was present. We mark these areas for future reference when we have encountered excellent fishing.

Flagging does not kill mature trees; in fact, it can help them. Cicadas have long been dubbed "nature's pruners" by biologists. The pruning of selective young growth on fruit-bearing trees is known to increase the yield and size of fruit. The cicada is drawn to the young branches and may contribute to the overall health of a tree. Just like their bodies are used as protein to feed the creatures that eat them, the cicada gives back to the trees, exactly the way nature planned. The cicada's life cycle is an example of nature's way of taking care of itself in harmony with purpose.

A Life Complete

At this point, the circle of life has been completed. All that is left is to allow the adults to fade away as the next generation begins its life's journey. The chorus noticeably lessens by the day, as the choir members fold their wings as well as their songbooks. The adult cicadas grow weaker by the day, as they age, deteriorate, and eventually perish. We have seen cicadas seemingly try to fight their impending doom by flying haphazardly, buzzing recklessly as if in a last-ditch effort to survive. During this time, we have found fishing activity is at its peak, with the greatest number of bugs flying, crashing, and burning on the surface of the water, and water-dwelling predators keyed in on them, constantly looking up for their next feast.

By this time, we have fished long and hard, often consecutive weeks on end. We've witnessed the changes in the sounds and sights, and the change in reactions of the fish to the bugs—from those first days of flying activity, with extremely willing and ridiculously easy-to-catch fish, to the days on the calendar reminding us that "it's almost over" as the fish become increasingly aware of fly pattern design, scrutinizing every bug or shying away from the ones that have a string attached. Soon the ground will be littered with the remains of cicada wings, and one day you will notice the chorus has sung its final notes.

By the time the eggs hatch, 8 to 10 weeks have passed and the adult cicadas are gone. We are left to wait with the memories and wonder of the fascinating event we were blessed to witness and hope to experience again beyond the next decade. If you are like me, you will find yourself scrolling through the memories, months—years even—between

Game over for the cicada that finds its way into the water when carp and other waterborne predators are keyed into their presence, but lucky for us when we can be present for the short and infrequent event. June 2020, Virginia.

emergences. With any luck, you are young, aware, and crazy about fly fishing, allowing you to have many more encounters with periodical cicadas and big, hungry fish. But in years that you are lucky enough to witness and fish a periodical emergence, you will likely still have the opportunity to fish during the annual cicadas' turn as summer blazes on.

ANNUAL CICADAS

The annual cicada contains the majority of the world's species of the insect. Over 150 identified species and 20-plus subspecies occur across the Lower 48 in addition to Canada and Mexico. These vary greatly in size and color, largely dependent on their local surroundings. Of these, a few localized species are of importance to the fly angler, particularly ones that emerge in the forests around fishable waters. The term "annual" is used to describe the nature of their occurrence, which means that members of the same species emerge every year. The underground life cycle of most annuals is two to nine years, with overlapping, unnamed broods emerging every year. Unlike the periodical, their emergence is not synchronized with the other members of their species. In some years, the emergences may seem greater than in others, much like "hopper plagues" in the midwestern and western states. This often confuses anglers, as many believe that western states have periodical cicadas because of years that had more prolific emergences than others. This is a protoperiodical condition, where emergences are prolific some years but scarce in others.

A few western species have been studied to better understand and hopefully crack the code to predict prolific emergences and better explain protoperiodicity. One of the studied species in particular is the *Okanagana*. A study of the species in California revealed that major emergence years typically depend on a precipitation threshold with a minimum developmental time component. This threshold is defined as 1,181

Female (left) and male (right) *Neotibicen linnei.*"

mm of precipitation after a minimum three-year period since the last emergence. More importantly, below the precipitation threshold, there were no significant emergences. The minimum three-year emergence period illustrates a linkage to the developmental growth required of the underground nymphs associated with precipitation, which directly impacts the cicadas' food source: xylem from vegetation. This ongoing study and others like it could provide clues to predicting peak emergences of other annual species (J. A. Cole and W. Chatfield-Taylor, Living rain gauges: Cumulative precipitation explaining emergence schedules of California protoperiodical cicadas. Ecology 98[10] [2017]: 2521–27).

Okanagana magnifica. Clues to this species' emergence may be related to rainfall. Found on the Green River in Utah, but also across the Pacific Northwest, this cicada is called the "mondo" for its size, or "buzzer" for the sound it makes. COLBY CROSSLAND

The *Okanagana magnifica* cicada, which is prominent on the Green River as well as many other rivers across the West, is one of these species, likely affected by cumulative rainfall but understudied in Utah. Anglers should pay attention and look for these clues that trigger an emergence. In my conversations with several longtime Green River guides, the explanation of the precipitation threshold seems to validate the observations on the river and during those years when the "mondos" were prolific and, more importantly, when they were not. It is, after all, a desert environment.

The life cycle, physiology, and habits of the annual cicada are otherwise similar to the periodical, save for a few interesting factors, which we will highlight.

The annual cicada's life starts much like that of its periodical cousin: It is born from one of the 500 to 600 eggs its mother laid in the bark of a young tree branch. From there, it falls to the ground in larval form and makes its way into the earth where it grows and develops, feeding on xylem sucked from tree roots. Depending on the species of annual cicada, it will grow to maturity, triggering emergence between two and nine years. There are no distinct, named, or geographically contained "broods" of annual cicadas. Because of this, there is every age class of nymph present in the soil every year. Depending on the previous year's breeding success, local climate, precipitation, and environmental factors, some years of emergence appear more prolific than others. These follow the normal predator-prey cycles like other insects and animals, as previously described. To our joy, as anglers, this means we get to see annual cicadas every year, however with the added uncertainty of "how good will it be?"

The Adult Annual Cicada

The evasion of predators for the annual is very different than for the periodical. For the periodical, the sheer numbers of insects ensure proliferation of the species. The annual has evolved without predator satiation abilities; rather, it depends on two factors: camouflage and flight. Across species, the annual cicada largely mimics the colors of its natural environment. Some are quite beautiful—greens and gold with whitish or gray backs that look like leaves, tree bark, or scales. Depending on their local environment, they tend to

Tibicen canicularis. The underside of this variety is predominantly white. Keep this in mind when designing and tying suitable fly patterns. DAVID STEPHENS, BUGWOOD.ORG

Tibicen canicularis, otherwise known as the "dog-day" cicada across the southern and eastern United States. DAVID STEPHENS, BUGWOOD.ORG

have evolved roughly copying the colors of the landscape they live in. Grassland cicadas are beige and tan, matching the dusty ground and landscape they emerge from, while southern and eastern cicadas match the lush summertime vegetation. In most cases, however, black, brown, and olive imitations with white, gray, or transparent wings and legs of black, tan, yellow, green, and orange will imitate most varieties.

Some species are hairy, with gray hairs over a black body giving them a dusty look, aiding in their camouflage. Remember, the fish-eye view sees a silhouette, largely a dark, wide abdomen ending in a point and either a narrow or splayed transparent wing shape. Colored legs imitate the legs as much as they do the wing shape. Keep this in mind when designing or tying patterns. The thick outer vein of a cicada's wing typically carries the color as variegated body segments or legs. One set of orange or tan-yellow legs and one set of black or clear legs can provide enough realism to match the hatch. Since annuals tend to live a bit longer in the final adult flying form, they also tend to vary in color as they age. Some species will retain their brilliant green or colored variegations, but others will often darken with time, appearing almost completely black with transparent wings by their end of life.

In addition to a wide array of coloration, the annual cicada has evolved to be an agile flyer, in both speed and direction. I have, on several occasions, found an adult annual cicada on a tree branch and tried to catch it with my bare hands. I have seldom been successful! They are very aware of their surroundings, and will flush when a potential threat gets nearby. They evade capture from land animals very easily. I have seen a family of mockingbirds chase and capture "flushed" dog day cicadas in my backyard with both failure and success. I would assume that birds are the exception to the flight-savvy annual cicada's ability to avoid becoming lunch, in addition to the unlucky bug that falls into the water as fish bait.

A male periodical *Magicicada septendecula* in Pennsylvania and a male annual *Platypedia putnami* in Utah. Note the similarities: body shape, coloration, wings, and eyes. Size between these two species is the most significant difference. The *septendecula* towers in comparison to the inch-long *putnami*

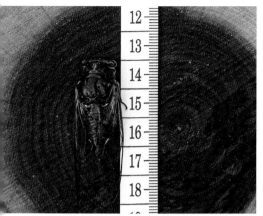

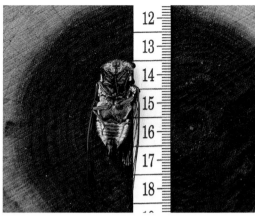

Neotibicen lyricen englehardti. This species is the blackest of all annual cicadas, with bright green outer wing veins. This is a male of the species; note the amber-colored "anchor" or "pull tab" marking on its head, and its wide body.

Neotibicen lyricen englehardti. This species has a frosty white belly with a distinct black streak in the center. Note also the tymbal covers. These are the tan-olive pads across the mid-section, below the last set of legs.

Okanagana magnifica. Note the gray eyes and robust body shape. COLBY CROSSLAND

Bottom side view of a *Neotibicen tibicen* male cicada. Note the silver-frosty white abdomen and golds and greens on the legs.

Okanagana magnifica. This is a female of the species. Note the profile, coloration, and hairy appearance. Many patterns that match the periodical varieties will also match this species, which is predominantly black with orange. Also note the rostrum, or beak. Adults seldom feed but will periodically drink during their final phase of life, which lasts up to eight weeks for annual species. COLBY CROSSLAND

The mating calls of the male annual cicada are varied, dependent on species as well. In most cases, the deafening choruses are absent; however, the calls can still be very loud and are concentrated in locations of peak mating activity. The types of sounds can vary from buzzes to clicks, based on the physiology of the particular species. For example, male "buzzing" cicadas possess the same anatomy as periodicals—tymbals located on their sides, just behind the wings. These are flexed and create a specific frequency to attract a mate of the same species. These calls are often loud and unmistakable in the high treetops. An interesting species of cicada that is of special interest to the angler is the crepitating *Platypedia* species. "Crepitation" is the technical term for rapid wing movements and flexing of wing veins to make cracking or popping sounds, much like cracking your knuckles. These are often called "wing banger" or "clicker" cicadas.

While they still use sound to attract a mate, the method is much different. A

Platypedia putnami: male on the left, female on the right. Note the female ovipositor that is partially exposed. This will extend after mating to be used to slit tree branches and deposit eggs. Note that the male lacks tymbal covers, as this species does not possess tymbals.

Platypedia putnami, "Putnam's cicada," also known as the "fisherman's friend." Found on the Green River near Dutch John, Utah, June 2022.

A brown trout fooled by a "clicker" cicada of the author's design on the Green River.

flicking motion of the wings makes a "clicking" sound, hence the nickname "clickers." These are a prevalent species across the Mountain West, specifically *Platypedia putnami*, or "Putnam's cicada." These are the small "clickers" that guides describe on Utah's Green River, Arizona's Colorado River at Lees Ferry, and across Colorado's Front Range during the middle of May to July. They occur annually in great numbers and are predictable enough to provide unforgettable fishing. This species in particular seems to favor stream-side trees and shrubs, which in turn favors fishing.

Most adult annual cicadas live as flying insects for about six to eight weeks. This is largely due to the time it takes to find a mate within its species that are not emerging like the synchronized periodical. The periodical emerges in huge numbers in a relatively short period of time. Most annual species emerge over the course of several weeks. They are around longer, which offers a benefit *and* a curse to the fly angler. The benefit is that because they are present in the environment for a longer time, there is more time for fish to have an opportunity to identify them as a food source and eat them. Fish will imprint on an infrequent big meal and tend to take the opportunity when it presents itself. This means that even when we might not see a lot of natural insects around, we still can have success fishing the patterns. This is no different from western hopper fishing. There are enough bugs around for a long period of time that fish will hold against banks and under overhanging grass, and take the opportunity to eat a hopper when it presents itself, even during mayfly, caddisfly, or aquatic insect hatches.

The potential curse is that those prolific years of epic cicada fishing can spoil the rest of the season's dry-fly fishing. This is often the case on Utah's Green River, where in years of great cicada fishing in May through July, the midsummer dry-fly fishing then gets extremely technical and difficult. The fish seem to get analytical toward any fly on the surface. Many have been accused of counting legs and turns of hackle!

CONSERVATION

As previously established, cicadas are one of the largest insect groups, with a wide, global distribution. The periodical species, however, while prolific, are isolated to their range in the eastern United States. They have evolved over millions of years in response to drastic and dynamic climatic shifts, natural events, and predatory evolution. Nonetheless, cicadas are not immune to the effects of humans on the environment. Possibly the biggest threat to cicadas is urban expansion. The cicada's life cycle is dependent on trees and the first meter of earth's topsoil. Urban expansion, suburban sprawl, and loss of natural spaces where trees are traded for parking lots and strip malls have reduced populations of cicadas globally. Such is the case of previous locations of Brood V near Long Island, New York, and Brood XIII in Illinois. Only remnant populations are believed to exist, where they may have once been prolific.

Pesticides used for insect management on lawns, fruit trees, and gardens likely have an impact, but probably not in deep woods where mature trees exist and typical chemical use is not present. Depending on the time of year when these are applied, there may be little effect because the immature insect is deep in the earth's soil; however, there will be some losses, though unlikely to destroy full populations.

A potential threat in the United States, first discovered in Pennsylvania but now spread across the East and Midwest is the spotted lanternfly. This insect made its way from Asia, likely in freight. In its native range wasps keep the species in check, but North America lacks this predator and has seen massive increases in spotted lanternflies. These insects are also a prolific species that possesses mouthparts that suck tree sap, not from roots, but from young growth on adult trees. In areas where the lanternfly is concentrated, they have the ability to stress mature trees. The deciduous forests of the East—the massive stands of black walnut, maple, ash, hickory, sycamore, and beech—all face a potential impact from this invasive species.

A second invasive species, the emerald ash borer, also native to Asia, has been in the United States for two decades. First identified in Michigan in 2002, it has spread to 36 states across the Midwest to the northeast. The beetle attacks all species of ash and has been responsible for decimating native ash tree populations where it is found. The adult beetle lays eggs between the bark and in crevices in the ash tree. The larvae hatch and burrow beneath the bark to feed. Not only does this stress the adult trees, causing bark splits, upper crown die-off, and disease, but woodpeckers find the larvae and cause significant damage to the trunk of trees in their effort to eat the immature phase of the insect.

Preserving green spaces, protecting trees, and stopping the spread of invasive species to allow for native plant species to proliferate, selective harvest of timber are the best environmental management practices for our friend the cicada. Now more than ever, our public lands are being challenged for their above- and underground resources, and we cannot forget about the cicada! The cicada holds significance for the environment through its own contributions as nature's pruner, an abundant food source for creatures big and small, and finally in its own death, returning to the earth to provide nutrients for microorganisms and plant life as it decomposes. Our environment—our world—would not be the same without the cicada.

Emergence Timing: Where? What? When?

For the annual species, timing the emergence can be a little trickier than for their periodical cousins. You need to know the geographical area you wish to find them in as well as the distinct species in that area. Some western annual cicadas begin to show up in the middle of May and peak in June. This is the case for *Platypedia putnami*, a small, orange-black-gray cicada found in Utah and Colorado. Others, like the *Tibicen canicularis*, *Neotibicen lyricen*, and *Neotibicen linnei*, or "dog-day cicada," found in the eastern states, begin to emerge mid- to late summer, often July through August. Some areas benefit from multiple species of annual cicadas as well. The *Okanagana magnifica* is a large western cicada that occurs in June and July in many states. This is the famous "mondo" cicada that sometimes shows up in the Green River in Utah riding the coattails of the smaller *Platypedia*.

The best way to approach planning to meet an annual cicada emergence is to research the area you plan to visit. Pick your destination and identify the rivers, lakes, and streams you wish to fish. First visit www.cicadamania.com and narrow your search to states. From there, you will be able to identify the common species in that particular state. Take note of the mating calls and listen for these sounds surrounding the waterways during scouting missions. Look up the insects' scientific name at the local agriculture extension office, museum, or university. I have had great success picking up the phone and talking to university scientists or museum curators. You will find they love when people take interest in their work! From here you should be able to identify the geographical range of the insect as well as find any research, studies, or reports on any scientific monitoring. By identifying the possible insects in that area, you know what you are going to need to imitate it and when to be there. Again, it is often not terribly important to match the natural exactly with size, shape, and coloration. Close enough is often good enough.

There are a few well-known destination fisheries that provide fantastic cicada fishing opportunities. Utah's Green River below Flaming Gorge and the Colorado River at Lee's

Neotibicen linnei. Note the curvature of the brilliant green outer wing vein. This is a key identifier of this species, which is common across many states in significant numbers from July through September.

Neotibicen tibicen: male of the species. This very common and important species of annual cicada is found in the Midwest, southern, and northeastern states.

Ferry are two popular tailwaters that are known to provide anglers with excellent and predictable annual opportunities. Note that these are tailwaters. The cicadas that occur on these waters happen to emerge in June. In western states, June is a temperamental time, with free-flowing rivers high and off-color from mountain runoff. Targeting tailwaters is a good bet for May, June, and the first half of July to miss runoff. During late June of 2022, Yellowstone National Park and the surrounding area suffered massive devastation from extreme flash flooding, with rivers rising to levels never before seen. During this same time, I spent a week on the Green and experienced epic fishing on cicadas in the gin-clear waters below Flaming Gorge. Look for cicada activity near tailwaters and mountain lakes to avoid runoff conditions.

Remember that cicadas are terrestrial, and therefore not limited to the drainage or waterway you may find them in. Often, they will be prolific across an area, on other nearby rivers and streams. You would do well to explore these and research other waterways for increased fishing opportunities and options when the river blows out or plans change. Localized emergences will likely occur during the same times as nearby waters.

Common Annual Species Found East and West

Most US states have 20 to 40 varieties of annual cicadas distributed across their landscapes. However, the exact species identification is often unnecessary. Again, much like the grasshopper, size, shape, and color are of importance to the angler. Below is a list of the more prevalent annual cicadas of interest to anglers.

GENUS	COMMON SPECIES	LOCATIONS	TIME	SIZE (BODY)	COLORATION	NOTES
Diceroprocta	D. apache	AZ, CA, CO, NV, NM, UT	June–August	23–25 mm	Black, tan, pale yellow-orange	Cicadas in this genus are often found in floodplains, near rivers and streams.
Diceroprocta	D. vitripennis	AL, AR, IL, IN, KS, KY, LA, MI, MS, MO, NE, OK, TN, TX, WI	June–August	21–23 mm	Green, black, and tan	Green wing veins and a green-tan underside
Diceroprocta	D. olympusa	AL, FL, GA, MS, NC, SC	June–August	21–23 mm	Brown, black, and tan	Called "scrub cicada" for its preference for small shrubs and medium-size trees
Megatibicen	M. auletes	AL, AR, CT, DE, CD, FL, GA, IL, IN, IA, KS, KY, LA, MD, MA, MI, MS, MO, NE, NJ, NY, NC, OH, OK, PA, SC, TN, TX, VA, WV, WI	June–September	30–35 mm	Olive, black, tan, and white	Largest of all North American cicadas
Megatibicen	M. pronatalist walkeri	AL, AR, FL, GA, IL, IN, IA, KS, LA, MD, MI, MN, MS, MO, NE, NC, ND, OH, OK, SD, TN, TX, VA, WV, WI, WY	July–September	30–33 mm	Leaf green, brown, and black with white	Green wing veins. Called "Walker's cicada." An important and prevalent species in the middle US states north to south.
Neo cicada	N. hieroglyphica	AL, AR, DE, FL, GA, IL, IN, KS, KY, LA, MD, MS, MO, NJ, NY, NC, OH, OK, SC, TN, TX, VA	May–August	22–27 mm	Green, bronze-tan, and black	Distinct wing markings and bronze-tan underside
Neotibicen	N. canicularis	AR, CT, DC, IL, IN, IA, KS, ME, MD, MA, MI, MN, MO, NE, NH, NJ, NY, NC, ND, OH, PA, RI, SC, SD, TN, VT, VA, WV, WI	July–September	27–33 mm	Black with green and brown. Camouflage pattern	Neotibicen cicadas are large, loud species commonly referred to as "dog day cicadas." Occurring in mid-to late summer in the East and South, they have a preference for mature deciduous trees and occur heavily along riverbanks.
Neotibicen	N. pruinosus	AL, AR, CO, IL, IN, IA, KS, KY, LA, MI, MN, MS, MO, NE, NC, OH, OK, PA, SC, SD, TN, TX, WV, WI N. winnemanna: DE, DC, GA, MD, NC, NJ, PA, SC, VA	June–August	27–30 mm		Called "scissor grinder cicada" for its call that sounds like a blade sharpened on a grinding wheel. A prominent cicada in the central to eastern US states. Similar to N. winnemanna, or "eastern scissor grinder," in most of the same range. Same fly patterns cover both.

GENUS	COMMON SPECIES	LOCATIONS	TIME	SIZE (BODY)	COLORATION	NOTES
Neotibicen	Lyricen englehardti	AL, CT, DE, DC, FL, GA, IN, IL, KY, MD, MA, MS, NJ, NY, NC, OH, PA, RI, SC, TN, VA, WV	July–August	32–35 mm	These are almost entirely black, with an amber-tan "anchor" on the top of their pronotum (top of the head). Their underside is white with a black streak in the middle. Green wing veins.	Called "lyric cicada" or "dark lyric cicada." Very similar in call to other Neotibicen cicadas.
Neotibicen	Linnei	AL, AR, CT, DE, FL, GA, IL, IN, IA, KS, KY, LA, ME, MD, MA, MI, MN, MS, MO, NE, NJ, NY, NC, OH, PA, SC, TN, VT, VA, WV, WI	July–September	32–35 mm	Black, green-amber camo pattern.	Called "Linne's cicada." Very prominent in Midwest and the Great Lakes region. Key identifier is a prominent or exaggerated bend in its outer wings.
Neotibicen	Tibicen	AL, AR, CT, DE, FL, GA, IL, IN, IA, KS, KY, LA, MD, MA, MI, MS, MO, NE, NJ, NY, NC, OH, OK, PA, RI, SC, SD, TN, TX, VT, VA, WV, WI	July–September	35 mm	Black and green	Called "swamp cicada" or "morning cicada." The males sing their song in the morning, usually as the sun hits high in the trees and warms them up from their slumber. Species likes to sing early and quit during the heat of the day. Will often sing again at dusk. A very common species in the Midwest, south, and northeast range of the United States.
Okanagana	O. bella	CA, CO, ID, MT, NV, NM, OR, SD, UT, WA, WY Also, Alberta, Canada	June	23–25 mm	Black with orange outer wing vein, legs, and ribbed underside	Called "mountain cicada" for its wide distribution in the Rockies both in US and Canada. Found in western conifers along streambeds. Yellowstone National Park has this species.
Okanagana	Magnifica	AZ, CA, CO, NV, NM, OR, UT, WY	June–August	31–35 mm	Grey, tan black. Hairy with pale orange highlights	"Mondo"-size cicada. Found on the Green River in Utah.
Platypedia	P. Putnami	AZ, CA, CO, ID, MT, NE, NV, NM, OR, SD, UT, WA, WY	May–July	18–21 mm	Black, pale orange, almost yellow-tan highlights	Called crepitating or "clicker cicada." Males are easily identified by the clicking sound they make. Prolific around rivers and streams; prefer shrubs and mountain junipers.

Scouting Before the Main Event: Cicadas on the Water

RESEARCH

When I first started to investigate emergences of periodical cicadas, the tools and information we have today were simply not available. When Robert Bell and I first started to research historical records and locations, we had to dig deep. We scoured through old newspaper articles and scientific white papers, and called university agriculture and extension offices to find information about the insects. Our sole purpose, as you probably have figured out by now, was to plan our days off from work, family commitments, and other complexities of domestic living with the peak occurrences of cicadas near fishable waters. In many cases, it involved first finding where the bugs were going to be, then locating water—rivers, lakes, and streams—which we may or may not be familiar with.

Left to right: Bob Bell, Steve Ludwig, and the author compare notes, strategies, and theories during lunch on the river. It looks like Steve found a target and is getting ready to strip line off the reel to make a presentation. Brood V, 2016.

In other cases, we marked our future calendars with the years of specific "Broods" on bodies of water we knew well.

In 1991, the internet was just on the verge of being "the next big thing." The term "World Wide Web" had been coined but was not really available for public use. At this time, we were still using floppy disks, dial-up connections, and picture-tube monitors in a largely text-based internet. You get my point: The "information age" was just beginning. This was also the year of emergence of Brood XIV, with a massive and widespread distribution across central Pennsylvania, an area hallowed as having the best wild trout fishing the state has to offer.

When Bob and I started to look for information, we almost totally relied on Penn State University's science department. I reached out to entomologists and visited libraries for clues as to where and when the bugs would occur. I found a scientific source that said something to the effect of "June 1991, just before summer solstice, the bugs were at their peak." I planned time off from work between June 10 and June 18 of 2008 in hopes of meeting the emergence. The previous weekend, we did a scouting mission to look for signs of impending emergence near our favorite trout fishing spots. We found few, but still had hope. By June 10—the start of our eight days in central Pennsylvania—bugs were everywhere. Fish were everywhere too, looking up, eating the giant insects.

Information availability has changed significantly since 1991. Each year, technology seems to double with no plateau in sight. With every passing year, our ability to consume data and records of all kinds exploded exponentially. It has become very easy to find emergence data on broods that occurred in the early 2000s. Our research has evolved from paper materials and combing through library microfiche, and is unlikely to revert! This is good news for anglers and science.

Scientists have used the public for information gathering on cicadas since the first time they were discovered. In 1843, a medical doctor and the authority on cicadas at

A better-than-average brown trout ate the cicada in broad daylight with the bugs screaming on the banks. For perspective, that fly is a 1½-inch cicada pattern! June 2008.

the time, Gideon B. Smith, placed an ad in several Maryland newspapers requesting readers to send dates and locations of cicada sightings in an effort to accurately map the boundaries of broods. In return, he offered his work on "the history of the most curious insect in the world." Dr. Smith was ahead of his time, using the public to "crowdsource" data collection on cicadas.

The modern parallel to this is the work of Dr. Gene Kritsky, dean of the School of Behavioral and Natural Sciences as Mount St. Joseph University in Cincinnati, Ohio. As he was preparing for the emergence of the Brood X cicadas, otherwise known as "the great eastern brood," he knew that he wanted to accurately map the distribution and range. Remembering Gideon B. Smith's crowdsourcing the public for data, he thought, "I wish there was an app for that." Cicada Safari was born. Dr. Kritsky secured funding for the development of Cicada Safari in partnership with the Center for IT Engagement at the university. This app lets smartphone users upload location, date, and time information in addition to photos of cicada sightings and activity. This enables pinpoint location, GPS coordinates, and visual proof of cicada activity, which has allowed scientists across regions to collaborate, identify, and accurately map the boundaries of broods in addition to better understand straggler broods and behaviors. For instance, during the Brood X emergence in south-central Pennsylvania, I drove past singing cicadas where Brood X cicadas *shouldn't* have been. Using the app, I was able to identify stragglers of a separate brood. The cicadas I encountered in this area were stragglers of the 17-year Brood XIV cicadas, emerging the expected four years early.

This kind of data is invaluable to scientists and anglers alike. As time and technology continues, we will have an even clearer picture of periodical cicada brood location and range, and a better opportunity for scientists to focus research on understanding straggler behavior. Much of what we know today about periodical brood distribution is based on years of observation, dating as far back as the 1700s. What has not been accurately accounted for are "shadow" broods of 4- and 1-year stragglers showing up around a dominant emergence. Cicada Safari changes this understanding profoundly. With the app, accurate identification and location information will not only improve knowledge of the boundaries of dominant broods, but also provide better understanding of straggler behaviors, leading to further insight into evolution and even identification of new broods. Cicada Safari is a relatively new tool, but for the Brood X emergence of 2021, it was a game changer in locating data instantaneously. According to Dr. Kritsky, he and his team fully intend to continue using the app for data collection on all occurring broods of periodical cicadas.

A quick internet search on the keyword "cicada" will without a doubt result in the website www.cicadamania.com, an extensive site created by Dan Mowgli in 1996 and dedicated to "the most amazing insect in the world." It is full of information about periodical and annual cicada species across the planet. The interactive features are what make it valuable to anglers. Much like the Cicada Safari app, visitors can log reports of sightings with their location, dates, and time in addition to video and photographs. Many of the reports are written, so you will need to scroll through reports, look at a map, and find the locations. I recall Bob Bell sending me a screenshot of a particular report that told us exactly what we were looking for when we were trying to figure out where to fish Brood IX in 2020 in southern Virginia. This area is unfamiliar to both of us, but we knew it was an emergence year for the insect. Bob had found a report from 2003 on the website stating something like the following:

June 8, 2003. I was at the boat ramp at Lake X and billions of weird bugs were making noise in the trees. I saw a carp swim by and eat one of the bugs that landed in the water. My son and I started gathering up the bugs and using them as bait and caught fish until our arms were sore.

When scrolling through the immense number of reports, look for these kinds of details. In addition, take note of neighboring locations and find where rivers, reservoirs, and lakes are. I make lists of towns reported and use Google Earth to locate them, zoom in, and find bodies of water. When you find multiple, localized reports in an area with 20-plus-year-old forested areas, green space, and a reservoir or lake, you can almost be certain you will find the bugs near enough to water. Use the powerful tools of the technology age to find bugs and fish!

Research for annual cicadas is much different. Being that they occur each year, albeit in smaller numbers, you still can successfully locate fishable numbers of bugs. Typically, however, the annual cicada has "boom" years and "normal" years, much like other insects. I have witnessed years of phenomenal hopper fishing on the Bighorn River in Montana, while other years there were fewer but still fishable numbers. In boom years, the insects emerge in greater numbers, dependent on not-so-certain science. A leading theory is that it could be egg and larvae survival rate from the previous generation's mating cycle or a number of environmental conditions that "lined up just right." Weather patterns, rain or drought, and predation cycles are all common hypotheses.

Regardless of the reason, the best way to research the fishable populations of annual cicadas is to understand which species exist in a particular region and know when they emerge. For instance, in Colorado's Front Range, *Okanagana bella*, otherwise known as the "mountain cicada," exists and emerges in the middle of June. The third piece of information is to find "where," Which is a little trickier and takes some doing, but there are a few sources for information. The first is, obviously, anglers. Ask fly shops and guides, and check stream reports. The second is to use the Cicada Mania website. The third, and where I actually start, is to reach out to any existing biology and, if one exists, entomology department at local universities in the area. I have placed several of these calls to universities and ended up having long and informative conversations about bugs! Scientists love and welcome the opportunity to discuss bugs with and educate the general public. In these conversations, I typically ask what major species of cicadas exist in the area and if any recent specimens have been collected. They will almost always have location cataloged with specimens. Locate those areas on maps, find nearby waterways, and go when the time is right!

As mentioned, destination fly shops and guide services are also great places to ask. The main attraction to Dutch John, Utah, is the Green River. Dutch John is home to several fly shops that specialize in guiding fly-fishing clients from around the world. Every guide and shop in town has bins full of their favorite cicada patterns in hopes of the appearance of cicadas in May and June. Many guides are booked a year in advance with clients who have experienced ridiculous fishing on the river with giant foam cicada patterns.

When I am planning summer trips to the West, I always check the mentioned sources for the possibility of a cicada hatch encounter. More than once the extra homework has paid off with big fish on the big bug!

SCOUTING

All the research to this point is done to build your plan. Scouting is where the time spent on the internet, phone, and apps tells you if you are on the right track. Whenever feasible, going to see for yourself will increase the odds of success in your favor. The research filters the options. For periodical emergences, all the success I and my fishing partners have had is a result of frequent "scouting missions." These are best described as "road trips with no expectation of fishing or catching." It is still very much a part of the data gathering.

I mentioned the 2008 Brood XIV emergence in central Pennsylvania previously, and can draw similar parallels to the 2019 Brood VIII in the area where I reside. I moved to the area in 2007, which was too late to have a personal account of the 2002 emergence. Asking around, neither did my neighbors. But all the research on the brood indicated that it was very likely cicadas would emerge right in my area. Fortunately, I am located very close to three flood control projects, all tributaries to the Allegheny River. Every day after work I would drive to the local lake and walk the shoreline, check the trees, and look at the ground for signs of emergence. On May 27, 2019, I was making my rounds and discovered a huge sycamore tree covered in newly emerged bugs from the night before. For certain, there would be more in the coming days. Each day, I returned to find more and more trees covered in the same manner.

Telltale signs of emergence: Nymphal shucks cling to trees, giving away clues that adult cicadas have emerged.

The first carp of the 2019 Brood VIII emergence.

The numbers were building as expected. I returned every day, and on June 6, the singing started. Bugs were approaching the peak critical mass when singing and flying commenced. On June 8, I stood on the bank overlooking the water and saw a pair of 10- to 12-pound golden blimps swimming just under the surface about 10 feet from the shoreline. This is atypical behavior for the bottom-feeding carp. I knew exactly what they were up to. A fallen cicada lay in their path, and I watched one of the fish casually find the bug and eat it. I ran to the truck and grabbed my 7-weight fly rod, pre-rigged–for this very moment—with a cicada. I returned to the spot and waited. The two carp circled back, I presented a single cast, and both carp accelerated to take a shot at my fly. In typical carp fashion when eating a bug off the surface, they hunted around with open mouths until my fly found a rubbery lip. When I lifted the rod to set the hook, the water exploded with the fish's immediate change in attitude as it sped off like a sled dog running the Iditarod for open water. As I was fighting the "golden bonefish," I may have looked around to see who witnessed my moment of greatness. Not surprised and incredibly gratified, I was completely alone. This was the first of several hundred carp in the next two weeks during the 2019 Brood VIII emergence. I'd have this all to myself for the coming weeks. The fishless scouting days had paid off!

The important takeaway is that nature happens fast, but also on its own schedule. Having the ability to return and experience the cadence of emergence as well as knowing the basic science of the insect is key. If you find a few bugs, likely the fishing will not be good right then, but being able to wait—however impatient you may be——and return later will pay dividends. When you return and find a growing number of bugs, you can be sure that there will be thousands more in the coming days.

On another scouting mission, this time for the 2021 Brood X emergence, I had found a certain lake that sits on the edge of where Brood X and Brood XIV might overlap. I found only one report from 2004 indicating cicadas at the lake. On May 30 I took a drive to scout numerous waterways starting well south of the lake, near the Maryland border.

It was early, and it also was during a string of unseasonably cool temps for late May. The signs of bugs were few. As I drove north, I stopped and scouted creeks and mature woods for bugs. Again, I found very few, but I was confident that they surely would be there, but maybe later than expected. I found a few test holes and mud turrets here and there. When I arrived at the lake, on the far southern end, I parked and walked along the woods' edge, looking for mature trees that would have been prime targets for egg laying 17 years earlier. I must have looked peculiar because a junior park ranger checking gates saw me and approached. She asked, "What are you looking for?" I quickly responded, "Bugs!" "Ohhhhhhhh, you mean *cicadas*?!" she replied. I almost gave myself whiplash as I turned my head her way to ask if she had seen any. She told me that there were tons of bugs at the northern end of the lake. That intel made my day and, frankly, led to the best fishing that summer. Another lesson learned. Stop and ask the people that have been around! Ask the locals! Needless to say, as I reached the farthest access point north, I found the bugs, by the millions. No singing, no flying yet, but it was a sure thing.

When June 3 rolled around, we returned, boat in tow, and I caught my first of hundreds of carp right at the boat ramp! About a week later, we had scouted from the north end to the south, and bugs had begun where I first looked the previous Saturday. The old adage, "Don't leave fish to find fish," usually holds true, but in the case of prolific cicada emergences, you might be able to extend the fun on huge lakes and drainages by locating new bugs at different times during the emergence. In this case, we were able to find feeding fish into July on the entire lake.

The sidebar relates an experience on the water, shared by Bob Bell during the 2020 emergence of Brood IX in southern Virginia. The waters fished were unfamiliar to Bob at the time, and his story shows that research pays off.

One of the author's favorite cicada patterns eaten by a trophy carp off the surface. Sight fishing + big fish + big flies = who could ask for anything more?

Show up Early, Stay Late

Contributed by Bob Bell

Mark and I were beginning to get frustrated! We had done our research, taken time off work, traveled eight-plus hours pulling our motorboat to find uncooperative fish. The weather was the problem. We thought we had planned accordingly. The timing should have been correct but the weather had thrown us a curveball. The week before we arrived, a cold front had settled over the area, dropping epic amounts of rain. We came very close to canceling the trip due to a number of factors. The first-wave "COVID-19 shutdown" was barely over, and the lake that had never flowed over the spillway was out of its banks and dumping thousands of gallons of water over its spillway! We stewed at home for a couple of days, but a call to the boat ramp revealed that the water was no longer going over the spillway and the boat launches were open. Also, with a little prodding, the guy at the launch said he could hear cicadas singing while we were talking! So we went and hoped for the best.

The cicadas were present, but due to the cold weather and rain, the emergence was delayed by several days. Because of this, few bugs were singing and, as a result, even fewer were flying. There were cicadas everywhere on the trees and vegetation, but we were not seeing very many on the water. In two full days of fishing, we were catching plenty of bluegills and a few spotted bass (a new species for us), but we had traveled this far for a species that pulled a lot harder than either of those. The carp we were after had not found the cicadas yet. We saw plenty of them, but they were acting like typical down-lookers sifting for foodstuffs in the muddy shallows. We had seen plenty of them in the high water near the banks of the lake, but they had not "noticed" the large protein meal on the surface yet.

The way it usually works is the aggressive, surface-oriented bluegills start to sample the cicadas as soon as they accidentally end up floating on the surface of the water. The bugs are too big for the bluegill mouths, so they drag them under and tear them into pieces and eventually eat them. This commotion gets the attention of the carp. The carp come over for a look and eventually steal cicadas from the bluegills. Over several days the carp begin to realize that

Bluegills are the early adopters of cicada eating. MIKE ENGELHARDT

the cicadas are on the surface and start looking for them on their own. On this lake the blue-gills had found the cicadas but the carp we had traveled for had not figured it out . . . yet! We decided to make a move. The lake we were fishing was at high elevation for the area, and it was in a narrow valley. We hypothesized that these factors would mean the cicadas here were in the lower-elevation areas that had lakes in the wide valleys with more warming sunshine and better ground temperatures.

We had researched other lakes in the area; the problem was that the other lakes were huge. Our hope was that there would be cicadas on them, but finding them was going to be challeng-ing due to the enormous size. We broke out the Cicada Safari app on our phones and started doing research over beers in the hotel room. This app allows users to take photos of cicadas when they see them. It even has a leaderboard to encourage competition for numbers of photos submitted. The great thing about this for anglers is when the cicada chasers take a cell phone picture of a cicada, the location of the photo is displayed on the map inside the app. Using the app, you can look at the map for the area you want to fish. On the map there is a small cicada icon for each photo taken at the specific location. It becomes a simple matter of finding bodies of water on the map within the app and then zooming in to the individual icons to find the cica-das on the edges or near bodies of water. All we needed was to see a single periodical cicada, knowing where there is one, there will be millions more. They don't live alone! Thanks to some Cicada Safari contributors, we found what we were looking for; there was a cicada population uploaded to the app, on one arm of the lake. With further looking on internet maps of the lake, we located the boat ramp nearest to the reports. Now we had a plan.

In the morning we would begin our search for cicadas near the water. Since this lake was at a lower elevation and was in a wider valley with more open slopes to warming sunshine, we reasoned that the cicadas had been out of the ground a couple of days longer here. We hoped that the late-to-the-party carp had found the bugs that were ending up on the surface of this giant lake.

The next day shortly after daylight, we arrived at the boat ramp near our destination. As the sun began warming the treetops where the cicadas were sleeping, we slowly motored our craft to the arm of the lake that had cicada reports. As soon as the noise of the outboard had quieted, smiles spread across our faces; there were bugs singing in the trees!

We dropped the trolling motor and headed for the loudest sound of cicadas singing in the trees. Slowly trolling along that shoreline, we caught a couple bluegills that recognized our imitation flies as real bugs. We had not found any carp yet. About 15 minutes into the shoreline cruise, it happened. Mark was on the trolling motor and I was standing on a cooler in the bow of the boat for increased visibility when I pointed to a large wake heading our way at 100 feet. Mark cut the trolling motor, and soon we could tell that it was three carp just under the surface, backs sometimes out of the water, hopefully hunting for cicadas. My cast dropped six to eight feet in front of the trio with a small plop, and they all raced to it! The first one there tipped up, whiskers out of the water, groping for the imitation. When my fly disappeared into the center of those orange lips, I gently raised the rod and was tied up to a complete donkey of a fish! It motored off with rip-roaring speed, dove deep, and showed me the forgotten color of the back-ing on my 8-weight fly reel. The long drive and all the research were well worth it!

The remainder of our trip followed similarly to finding that first trio of fish. It became a hunt. A hunt for bugs and fish. Now knowing where we had bugs and fish, the pressure to find more was off. We would scout new areas, and find other parts of the lake that had fresh fish and loads of bugs as well as areas seemingly absent of the critters. This clued us into how spotty the bugs can be at times, especially on huge bodies of water. You have to be mobile. Find the bugs, and they will lead you to fish.

We found carp cruising the surface looking for cicadas that had mistakenly gotten into the water. The mating clusters were on points, tucked back into little coves where mature trees reached the edge of the water. There were enough bugs to encourage fish to cruise the edges

Bob Bell with the first of many carp that would rise to smash cicadas in Virginia. June 2020.

looking for a meal. We explored other areas of the lake, going to and from the boat ramp, but nowhere else did we find mating groups of cicadas. Cicada Safari had helped us by narrowing down our search for bugs near the water. Spend your time fishing where there are bugs. The fish in other areas will not recognize the cicadas as a meal, and you won't find them on top hunting for cicadas.

After two amazing days fishing on the big lake during the middle of the week, the weekend had arrived. We knew this would bring out significant recreational boat traffic, as it was a very popular area for water-skiers, Jet Ski riders, and wake-surfers, being an unrestricted horsepower lake. This would mean waves would crash the banks and make the first 10 to 15 feet of the shore muddy. In addition to lack of clarity, we would likely have to contend with significant wakes and swells in our comparatively tiny 18-foot jet boat. This made us wonder: Had the carp from the first lake found the cicadas on the surface? Would they be hunting and targeting the big bugs that ended up in the water? Only one way to find out.

We went back. From our first couple of days fishing this lake, we knew where the largest concentrations of mating cicadas were located. We launched and ran quickly to the closest location that we knew had lots of cicadas. As we cut the motor and quietly drifted in, we could see several carp in the skinny water along a sandy beach-like bank. These fish were moving steadily on the miniature flat, seemingly hunting in the shallow water near some overhead trees. It was Mark's turn to swing a fly, so he made a single cast in front of a fish in about six inches of water.

This fish heard or felt the fly drop and casually cruised over to it. Without hesitation, it confidently tipped up and ate Mark's fly like it was paid to do it. After a couple of days of practice with surface-feeding carp on the big lake, Mark's skills were on point; he gently raised his rod and the carp did what they do when hooked: pull hard, run away with all your fly line, and head for deep water for five or six minutes before turning over and sliding into the net. The carp on this lake had finally found the floating T-bones that littered the shoreline. We had three more days of fishing on this lake, with easy and willing carp, bass, and bluegills anywhere we found cicadas near the water—what a great trip we had!

Fish Behavior: Carp, Trout, Bass, and Beyond

"DID YOU SEE THAT?" BOB EXCLAIMED WITH EXCITEMENT AS HIS ROD bent and line peeled off the reel. We were fishing a little-known lake in southern Virginia during the Brood IX emergence of 17-year cicadas. A bluegill attacked his imitation on the surface but couldn't get the giant size 4 foam fly in its tiny mouth. The fish swam off with the bug underwater while its pals followed it around trying to nip a bite of the giant fly. Bob didn't yet set the hook because he could almost sense what happened next. A carp was oddly hanging around the group of panfish, displaying aggressive behavior by erratically circling the fish beneath an overhanging multiflora rosebush where cicadas were singing. The carp noticed the bluegill with the imitation food in its mouth and suddenly charged the fish, full-on Donnybrook style. The bluegill, swimming for its life, let go of the fly, and the carp inhaled it right from its mouth.

This is the kind of occurrence you will find early in the emergence. The ever-curious bluegill is always looking at the surface for food items, while the bottom-feeding carp is doing the same, subsurface. The carp seized the opportunity to steal that meal from the poor bluegill, but where did this big, tasty, protein-packed insect come from? The

A brown trout fooled by a cicada pattern

45

carp—and all the other fish—would soon find out. In general, all fish species will exhibit some sort of learned behavior throughout the cicada emergence.

In the range of North America where cicadas emerge, the existing fisheries are highly diverse—warmwater, coldwater, tailwaters, free-flowing rivers, mountain streams, and man-made impoundments. While all the fish species in these waterways will eat a cicada, there are target species that seem to prefer, and even hunt, the insect.

TROUT

The fish that most often comes to mind in the fly-fishing world is the trout family. This fish of supreme elegance, beauty, diversity, and significant range often holds a special place in anglers' hearts. They seem to refuse to live and thrive in ugly places. They certainly are a "helluva lot prettier than they need to be," as John Gierach writes. Their eating habits are a perfect fit for dry-fly fishing, and they even demonstrate a preference to hold a position in the river, "looking up" and selectively rising to the surface for food, which makes for some really exciting visual experiences.

The native species distributed widely east of the Mississippi is the brook trout. Since the late 1880s, non-native species, namely the brown trout and rainbow trout, have been stocked in likely every waterway that holds fish. In the West, cutthroat trout and rainbows are the native species, with hybrids of the two along with brook trout and brown trout occurring in many of the renowned waters for a century. For the sake of discussion, we will refer to "trout" as a general grouping of the fish species. During a cicada emergence, they will react to the insect in the same way.

The trout's inclination to eat on the surface makes it an outstanding fish to target during a cicada emergence. Trout are often some of the first fish species to take notice of the cicada. Part of this has to do with the trout's physiology. The location of the eyes plays a specific role in how the fish will see a natural or imitation insect. A trout has a binocular peripheral vision to the surface that is about 97 degrees. This is referred to as its

"cone of vision." For example, a trout sitting on the bottom of a 2-foot-deep streambed has a cone of vision of approximately 6 feet. Looking at the surface is quite a natural thing for a trout; put simply, they're designed for it. And it serves them well.

If you compare a size 16 Pale Morning Dun mayfly with a 2-inch-long cicada, it's obvious the trout has no problem finding the cicada in any water type. In fact, it sees either bug very well. In addition, the trout's cone of vision at the surface is refracted, enabling a view wider above the water. It notices things like trees, birds in flight, and anglers standing on the bank of a river.

In contrast to aquatic insect hatches, where the trout inhabits the same eco-system as the entire life cycle of water-borne insects, it is only "by accident" that it takes notice of the cicada. The cicada,

Steve Ludwig with a well-fed rainbow trout during Brood V, 2016

Sometimes the trout that eat cicadas are as long as your arm.

being terrestrial for its entire life cycle, is only accidentally in the trout's environment. Worlds collide.

And when the periodical cicada emerges, it's right on time for the trout. Typically, by late May to the end of June, the great eastern mayfly, stonefly, and caddisfly hatches have passed. The vegetation is lush, terrestrial insects are in their adulthood, and trout have switched from "keyed" eating habits of predictable aquatic hatches to opportunistic feeding. For the fly angler, things get tougher; by now the fish have more experience with avoiding predators. That is, until the cicada arrives. I have found that trout will set up in all areas of a river or stream once keyed on the insect. They will often lie in a 2- to 3-foot-deep slot under clear water conditions so they can have a larger cone of vision of the surface.

The cicada ends up in the water at random. The deep-setting trout will scan the surface from below and aggressively react to the surface disturbance of the large insect hitting the water. This results in explosive takes that will help the angler locate fish in addition to making a quick hookset. There is often no mistaking that the trout ate your fly! Early in the emergence, trout will rarely, if ever, eat a cicada discreetly.

Trout will also cruise or hang in shady spots. This is a learned behavior: hide in the shadows, avoid predators from above. And they will eventually learn that the shady spot is because of a tree, and that tree seems to continually provide food as a result of the clumsy flying cicadas falling into the water to meet their unfortunate demise as a fish's meal. Trout will often attack as a reaction to an aggressively placed fly. Dead drifting with an intermittent twitch or mend produces excellent results.

Colby Crossland with a well-fed rainbow on the Green River. Fish were keyed on the smaller patterns during this trip in June 2022.

On the Green River in Utah, guide and fly tier Colby Crossland also shares insight on pressured trout. The Green is home to two prominent species of annual cicadas that occur from late April through July: *Platypedia putnami* and *Okanagana magnifica*. The trout in this gold medal fishery hunt the bugs and attack them with reckless abandon early in the hatching cycle. However, days later, they too become hip to the bugs that sting. Colby shares that quite often trout will nip a leg of a fly, drag it underwater, and wiggle it to see if it is real. He also said that in big cicada years, it almost ruins the remainder of dry-fly fishing for the season. The fish learn fast!

A 14-inch dissected brown trout, with its entire stomach contents consisting of cicadas, illustrating how trout will continuously feed on available cicadas. STEVEN MEANS, AQUATIC BIOLOGIST, DEPARTMENT OF ENVIRONMENTAL PROTECTION

With these pressured fish, realistic true-to-size patterns and the ability to present the fly in a lifelike manner is critical to getting an eat. In addition to realistic patterns, downsizing imitations often is enough to trigger a strike from over-pressured fish. Cody Eardley, a schoolteacher and fellow wooden boat builder, also spends his early summer looking for trout eating cicadas on the Green River. He recommends a downsized pattern, and has adapted Charlie Craven's Baby Boy Hopper into a black-and-orange cicada color scheme in sizes 10 and 12 to imitate the inch-long clicker cicada that is prominent in June on the river. He continues to fish this pattern long after the cicadas are gone, to great success. You can find this pattern adaptation in the fly-tying section in chapter 5.

All fish metabolize food relative to water temperature, oxygen, and age. Trout rely on cold, clean, and moving water to survive. They have a high metabolic rate, as they consume energy in current and cooler water—expelling energy for feeding. This means they need to continuously search for food. Because of this, they seem to eat cicadas long after the emergence has passed. Since the cicada emergence occurs around the longest days of the summer, there's a cautionary tale here, too. Longer days mean elevated water temperatures for trout, which adds additional stress. Always take the water temperature, and fish early or late in the day—or better yet, target other species during times of high heat. Try to limit targeting trout at water temperatures above 65 degrees F.

Another consideration for the health of the trout is to use barbless hooks. Cicada patterns range from #12 to #2, and especially with the larger-size patterns, the hooks become potentially lethal, for both small and large fish. On small fish, large hooks may inflict eye and gill damage, as well as tear the jaw. On larger fish, trout that eat aggressively will inhale the fly, and it often gets hooked on the tongue, or deeper in or near the gills. Consider using a size smaller barbless hook, or a light wire hook with an easily pinchable barb. Many of the patterns in chapter 5 call for these options. Fine wire hooks, barbless, or hooks with micro-barbs that can be pinched easily are recommended. You will also find that many of the patterns listed as size 4 long-shank hooks when compared with a natural are actually about a size smaller. The natural could be tied on a size 2, but is just as effective on a size 4 long-shank. Fish do not notice a difference. You may actually find a better hookup ratio in the mouth of an average trout with a smaller hook, as well.

Despite a large trout's size and big jaw, a smaller hook might prove more effective and do less harm. Also be aware that not all the fish will be of monstrous size when fish are targeting cicadas. Lots of smaller fish can be harmed by large hooks.

BASS

I texted Blake a photo of the menu at the restaurant I was sitting in while having dinner with my wife in late August. "Have you ever seen that beer available outside the state of Vermont?" I asked him, referring to Heady Topper, an IPA of legendary stature from the Alchemist brewery in Vermont. "Are you in Vermont?" he quickly wrote back. "Nope. You been fishing?" I asked him next. "No, but I'm off daddy duty tomorrow so I'm going somewhere." I had already planned to be on the river, and wouldn't you know, there was space in my boat. Blake can cast *and* he can row. We quickly made plans to meet at my house at 8 a.m. With the fishing having been the way it was yesterday; I anticipated a great day chasing smallmouth bass on surface cicada patterns.

Blake showed up, as he always does, a couple minutes on the early side of right on time. I had the boat hitched and ready to roll, and a fresh pot of coffee brewed. We shook hands, threw his gear in back, and headed for the river. The day was forecast to be just about perfect—hot weather and great river conditions, and we were planning a long float to put us on prime water midday. Fishing with friends like Blake is an enjoyable experience. It's predictable. It's laid-back. Blake has a genuine love of fishing, and since he doesn't get out that often being a new dad, he takes every opportunity and makes the most of it. He giggles every time he sets the hook on a fish. He likes to row a boat as well. He might even say he likes to row as much as he likes to fish. If you own a boat, keep friends like Blake around. I ran the shuttle, and as I rode my bike back to the put-in, I could see Blake casting long to the edge of the riffle from the last bridge crossing. He had all the rods rigged, the boat organized and he was ready. As I arrived, he already had landed three fish. It was going to be a heck of a day.

It's customary to give the guy who ran the shuttle first casting rights, and I'll admit, I did feel a little guilty. But the water ahead was only so-so, and I promised myself I'd row after the first fish or once we reached the first rock garden, where the fishing really gets good. I'd have to give up the rod for the sticks after only the first few casts. No problem, not a time to get greedy. Blake drove a long way, and I have been fishing like a fiend lately. His turn.

The rest of the day was just typical late-summer fishing—low-ish summer flows, hot and humid with little air movement, annual cicadas singing in the sycamores along the river. As the morning headed toward noon, the tubers and inflatable mattresses made their way to the river for "lazy river" beer drinking floats. You are hardly alone during the heat of summer. It's quite all right, and often downright entertaining at times. Play your cards right and you might get tossed a cold one or two. There's room for everybody.

By the time we got to the section I anticipated fishing the most, we had already boated several fish, including some very good ones. We both fished surface patterns like Flip Flop Cicada Poppers, Summer Screamer Cicada annual patterns, cork-bodied creations, and Sneaky Pete variants. All of our flies caught fish. I dropped my Summer Screamer Cicada toward the bank at the end of a long downstream cast while talking Blake through the tactic of "cast long and don't twitch," when a better than average smallie sucked my fly off the surface in a vortex that looked like a flushing toilet, supporting my theory of "the fish know your fly is there, you don't need to twitch it." We both whooped and hollered with excitement as the fish ran straight to the boat, heading for the deeper cover behind us. I got tight to the fish, with Blake at the ready with the net. In a single efficient scoop, he had the fish in the net just as the barbless pattern slid free. "A little over 17 inches" Blake said as he measured the fish while I got my camera ready. "Did you see

Summer smallmouth bass love looking up for annual cicadas.

that eat?!" I exclaimed. "See that! It wanted the bug—no twitch!" After a quick snap, I released the fish and said, "You're up" as I made my way to the rower seat. We put a few more decent fish in the net, and shared lots of laughs on the hits, misses, and happenings of the day. I did notice Blake was letting his popper ride a little longer with fewer pops the rest of the float. I think the old man might have showed him something.

All bass are fantastic surface-eating fish. For as long as people have been fishing for them, surface takes—whether from conventional tackle or flies—have been among the most exciting ways to catch them. The main types of bass we will refer to here are the largemouth, smallmouth, and spotted bass. All will target the insect in similar fashion, just like the trout. Bass are always opportunistic. They are excellent hunters and will switch their preferred food source to whatever is available: frogs, damselflies, insects, crayfish, baitfish.

Much like trout, bass are equipped with excellent vision and a strong lateral sensing ability to detect motion. This makes them a great candidate for fishing flies with an aggressive "splat!" on the water to attract attention, similar to "ringing the dinner bell." Twitching flies, then pausing and waiting for the take is an exciting way to catch bass.

In rivers during June, bass tend to congregate in more oxygenated areas and places with structure, creating ambush spots. They will wait for their food source to come by, then they'll attack. This presents a unique opportunity when fishing for

A lake-caught largemouth bass on a cicada.
ROBERT BELL

A southern spotted bass on a cicada pattern. ROBERT BELL

them. I have seen bass in shallows where baitfish are present, with cicadas on the surface, and the bass are chasing the baitfish. They seem to shift their preference—or operate on a balanced diet!

Early in the periodical emergence, when the insects are just starting to show up on the water, bass seem to readily eat them. For anglers, this is an excellent opportunity for a scouting mission. You may have a handful of great days where bass eat the bug recklessly, then seem to shut off. We've made a number of observations and theories on why bass might shut off to periodical cicadas. In a conversation with Mike Engelhardt, fly-fishing guide with Laurel Highlands Guide Service, we discussed the smallmouth bass and our several experiences with periodical emergences. Mike is one of the handful of anglers I personally know who is about as crazy for cicadas as I am. In discussing bass, Mike raises a good point to ponder considering the timing of the periodical cicada. It occurs sometime in the very end of May, with the peak number of flying cicadas around June 10 or 11. At this time, the smallmouth bass in our local rivers are coming off the spawn. This, of course, doesn't happen all at once, trickling off over a period of a few weeks. It could be that the end of spawning is a recovery time for the fish, and they are still not very interested in eating heavily yet. Depending on the locale, the bass may be entering or leaving spawning season.

I spoke to Joe Brancato, aquatic biologist for the Pennsylvania DEP, about bass behavior as well. Joe is an expert in aquatic biology, fish, insects, and mussels as well as a dedicated smallmouth bass angler. In his work, he has dissected thousands of bass. He finds that at any time of year, crayfish are almost always present in the bass's stomach. Crayfish are unique creatures as well, and some interesting changes happen to them during this time of year. First, in order to grow in size, crayfish go through a series of molts, typically five or six times throughout their life. During the molting cycle, the crayfish is soft shelled and extremely vulnerable to predation, typically requiring them to seek refuge and hide. I have seen significant numbers of molting crayfish during early summer, a possible clue to the meal preference of the bass during this time. Second, the abundance of juvenile crayfish is high in May and June as egg laying occurs in early spring and hatching, development, and growth fall right in time for early summer. In general, in May through July, peak numbers of crayfish inhabit the underwater environment, and it could be that the bass are keyed on them, preferring them to the cicadas found on the surface.

A second theory is that bass are such efficient hunters that they quickly gorge on the overabundance and subsequently they may not eat every fly that floats by. The bass is always hunting, always in position for ambushing a meal. They may simply get full on the bug and stop eating for periods. Their opportunistic nature and curiosity seem to trigger eating, rather than a keyed behavior of searching for the insects. I prefer to fish a lot of my favorite bass spots early in the cycle and switch to other species when it is well underway. Bass can often be an unexpected bycatch when targeting other species that inhabit the same waters.

In addition to these theories, there are thoughts about night fishing for bass.

We pulled up to the boat ramp at sunrise to get an early start to our day of finding fish willing to eat cicadas. As we descended the hill to the lake, we encountered a traffic jam of trucks and boat trailers. Approaching the ramp, we quickly found that it was anglers taking out rather than putting in. As we waited for our turn at the ramp, we talked to a fellow fisherman de-rigging his boat. He informed us that there was a nighttime bass tournament on the lake and that the surface bite at night was excellent. So it could also be that during the hot days when periodical cicadas occur, bass move deeper to stay cool and feed on the surface under the cover of darkness and cooler water.

The annual cicada bass experience is quite different. The story at the beginning of this section highlighted a recent memory of bass fishing late-summer annual cicadas. In terms of annual cicadas in the East, Engelhardt notes that in late August when the "dog-day" cicada is present, albeit in lesser numbers, the fishing can be fantastic. "We often catch our best fish of the year. Float any black bug dead drift through likely spots and some of the best fish in the river will rise for the take." It is a bit slower time than the periodical emergence, but the rewards can be just as great. The key is casting long, and dead drifting a large, black or dark-colored popper or cicada under trees along the banks. You may be tempted to twitch or pop the fly, but dead drifting tends to provide explosive results. Sneaky Petes or the Chuck Kraft Excalibur pattern in size 2 or 4 is an excellent choice for this time of year, as is the Flip Flop Cicada Popper or Boogle Bug in black, olive, and white. Blue is also popular this

Bob Bell with a smallmouth that was out hunting cicadas in the cooler early morning. BOB BELL

A 17-inch smallmouth bass that fell for a dead-drifted cicada pattern at midday

time of year, however, not imitating the cicada directly, but the damselflies that are at their peak this time of year as well. For a more realistic cicada pattern, try Chocklett's Cicada or the Summer Screamer Cicada.

In the East and South, several varieties of annual cicadas sing in mid- to late summer every year along rivers, lakes, and throughout forests. These are an important and abundant food source, typically until the last bugs sing in September. At this time of year, there are less regularly occurring hatches and fish become a bit more opportunistic. In high-pressured areas, they are also a bit more educated. This time of year, the rivers we fish are often a bit lower than during spring and early-summer flows, and fish will often be in surprisingly shallow water. This makes them highly attuned to a bug falling on the surface, but also sensitive to sloppy casting, as well as the push of water from a drift boat or raft too close to the bank. Casting long helps, but be aware of line control; takes are often immediately when a fly hits the water. Trust the long, dead free drift!

Fishing in the middle of the day, when bugs are most active, seems to trigger a decent surface bite. In recent seasons, I spent several days on the water at all times of day—morning, middle of the day, and evening. By far, the most productive time for surface activity was the middle of the day. Cicadas are singing in the trees in the hot sun, sometimes trying to cross the river, and smallies circle beneath them waiting for a mouthful.

In addition to small and largemouth bass, pay attention to lakes and rivers that have striped bass or hybrid striped bass/white bass. In places that harbor these species, they can often be found cruising a shoreline, hunting for cicadas, smashing them on the surface like trout! Surely an experience you will want to have for yourself!

BLUEGILL AND PANFISH

Another "early adopter" of the cicada is the ever-present bluegill and its related cousins, warmouth, pumpkinseed, green sunfish, and a host of hybrids. This family of fish is equipped with a tiny mouth and a big appetite. They inhabit areas of slower-moving to still water and a variety of structure. Because of their tiny mouths, they are often surface eaters, sampling everything that falls into the water. Because of this, they are among the first to detect the presence of cicadas in lakes and ponds.

The cicada is often too big for a bluegill to eat in one bite, so what you will often see is a group of bluegills attacking a natural insect and dragging it from the surface to

Arguably the prettiest of panfish, the pumpkinseed

a shallow depth. The group will all get a bite or two. The bluegill does something else by exhibiting this behavior: It notifies other fish of the availability of this food source.

This "lightbulb" went off for us while fishing an emergence in southern Virginia. In the beginning of this chapter, I highlighted a fun memory. We were fishing a lake in southern Virginia for bass and carp during the 2020 Brood IX emergence. Cicadas were just beginning to make their mating noise, screaming on the hillsides, flying in the air, but there were limited numbers making their way to the water's surface. We caught few of our target species.

We saw plenty of bass and carp cruising around the shallows, seemingly looking for something. But we also noticed that wherever there were bluegills, we'd see small bass and carp. The early adopter bluegill would drag the cicada from the surface—as the bug was too big for its tiny mouth—and a carp or bass would swoop in to steal the meal! This was often extremely aggressive behavior. This lasted about a day until the carp finally had their own lightbulb moment and figured out the bugs were coming from the surface. Flies that were waterlogged, weighted, or dragged beneath the surface film would get noticed by carp. The other learned behavior from

Mark Stanley with a pumpkinseed hybrid caught on a cicada pattern. Bluegill and panfish provide constant dry-fly fishing wherever they are found. BOB BELL

the bluegill was that it would avoid the bugs when the carp were present. They seemed to dislike having their meals stolen! If you have the desire to fish for bluegills intentionally, downsize your periodical imitations to a #6 or #8 and have fun!

CARP

We pulled our drift boat to the shore and into the shade to take a break and have lunch. A landowner on the bank of the river walked over to talk with us. He was an avid bass fisherman and had lived on the banks of the river his entire life. We all had the glow of a good day of fishing. We had just released 20 or 30 carp in the 10- to 15-pound class, all on cicada flies. From his vantage point he couldn't tell what we were catching. Imagine his look of disgust when we answered his question "What are you guys catching?" with "*carp!*" He looked confused and surprised when he asked, "Why would you want to catch those ugly things?" Our response was simple: Who doesn't like catching fish measured in double-digit pounds, on the surface with an 8-weight fly rod in hand? When I think cicadas, I'm almost always thinking carp. Most of my cicada fishing friends agree. Cut to the chase and let's go fish carp! For fly anglers, carp are notoriously hard to fool when they are looking down in the mud. But when keyed on cicadas, they become quite possibly the finest dry-fly gamefish to pursue.

Common carp are non-native where they exist in North America. They are among the most widely distributed species in the world. We won't get into the eradication of invasives and preservation of native species; carp are here and likely to stay. To a fly fisher, they provide a challenge of tactic and tackle, and will test the stoutest of hooks, tippet, and gear. They have a high temperature tolerance, and fishable populations are likely located very close to where you are right now, reading this. They are a fantastic fish to chase when the summer temperatures make it dangerous to fish for the more temperature-sensitive trout.

The carp is an odd one when it comes to surface fishing. Opposite of the trout, the carp has a very poor cone of vision as a result of its physiology. With down-looking eyes and poor distance vision, they are equipped to excel as bottom feeders. Unlike the trout, the carp needs to hover just below the surface, often with their back out of the water, in order

There's nothing like the carp eating on the surface when cicadas are around.

The carp's mouth is built for big dry flies.

Robert Bell guiding an angler to lead the carp

to detect an insect on the surface. This provides us with incredible sight-fishing opportunities. Carp are also unique in that they do not possess a stomach. Their "gut" basically begins at their mouth and ends at the anus. In their digestive system, they have complex enzymes that enable them to quickly process their meals. They are super-digesters and built for large volumes of food intake from a variety of sources. This allows them to feed diversely and voraciously.

The carp is the "hunter" when it comes to fishing with cicadas. They will often cruise shorelines, as singles or in packs or groups, where they have been conditioned to be presented with food. We will often set up on a bank where the bugs are close to the water and watch. You will see disturbances on the surface: carp lips, backs, or explosions from eats. Fishing from a boat where you have a high vantage point and can see the fish against a light bottom is a great way to target them. Scan for incoming fish and present a fly ahead of them, about three to five feet. They will often locate the bug, swim under it, then turn and tip up to "find" it with their mouths.

The first few (or few hundred) times this happens, don't set too soon. The carp needs to tip up to eat off the surface, and it is completely blind at this point. It eats the fly by feel. When the fish closes its mouth, now set the hook firm and get ready for it to rip! Colby Crossland, the guide on the Green River, Utah, shares a great guide hack with his clients on not rushing the hookset. When a fish eats the fly, say "God save the Green" and then set the hook. This works for all rising fish, trout included!

In addition to the common carp, there is also the "grass carp," or white amur. These fish can reach four feet in length and are truly herbivores. To the fly angler, they are notoriously difficult to fool on the fly. A pond nearby my home was stocked years ago with sterile grass carp to control weed growth. I played with these fish for three years before finally getting one to eat a ridiculous imitation of a sycamore seed. Grass carp are incredibly wary, and known for unbelievable power on their first run. You can sometimes find them in golf course ponds and parks, and some escapees make it to rivers and lakes. When cicadas are on, the grass carp will eat them with reckless abandon. It may be your once-in-a-lifetime shot to catch an "easy" grass carp!

Where carp are pressured or have been caught before will also add an interesting element to the game. You will see the adaptation in their behavior toward imitations of the bugs. Much like a dog that has been previously stung by a bee, they will approach with caution, often bumping a fly to see if it flutters, or balking at the last second to refuse it.

The author with a good-size common carp on a cicada pattern. June 2019, western Pennsylvania.

Grass carp taken on a floating cicada imitation during Brood IX in southern Virginia

Father and son Robert and Chase Bell are all smiles with a blimp of a carp. This fish was Chase's first experience with cicadas and carp. June 2019, Pennsylvania.

When these fish are facing you, deciding whether to eat your fly, time seems to stand still. Their pectoral fins dance, their eyes seem crossed, and their whiskers and mouth work in concert to try to do the risk analysis if *this one bites back*. When they do eat, you and your friends will surely hoot and holler as you set the hook with the fish blazing like a runaway train, knowing the consequence of its decision. When they don't eat the fly, they often blow up on the fly as you set the hook anyway, resulting in a spray of fly line back toward you, causing you to flinch to avoid the size 4 hook in the face. The technical term for this is "whisker f—ed," referring to the sensory anatomy that looks like a moustache or whiskers on the mouth of a carp and the fact that the fish quite literally is flipping you the bird as you farm it hard, leaving you with an acre of heartache as it blows up and refuses your offering. While I don't exactly recall which of my friends coined the phrase, it was surely Bob Bell, Steve Ludwig, or Wade James on that film shoot in 2016 for Brood V, as we laughed and giggled like schoolboys while teasing each other for the countless hits and misses by the epic number of carp eating the bugs.

Even pressured carp that are keyed on the surface can often be caught with a better presentation and imitation. Downsize your fly, try a fresh one, or change to a finer tippet to avoid refusals. However, carp are often abundant. A winning tactic is to search out new areas to find willing fish, or give them a rest. They often return to areas known to have food.

OTHER SPECIES

As with the previously discussed fish, almost every fish that swims will take notice of the cicada at some point in the emergence. I have witnessed catfish, bowfin, suckers, fallfish, chubs, pike, and pickerel find and eat cicadas. It is my experience that most of these fish eat with opportunity but don't develop a preference for the insect. Observe the surface and surrounding landscape, scout waterways, and know the major fish populations. For instance, in areas where bowfin are prolific, their abundance will force them to take opportunities to eat whatever food items are available. Find the bugs near a waterway, scout that waterway, and chances are you will find multiple species that will rise to the cicada. Sometimes, the interesting bycatches are the most enjoyable!

Great Destinations: Notes for Success

IN WRITING THIS BOOK, I WANTED TO GIVE THE READER INSIGHT AND understanding of the cicada emergence and share the tools to find their own local and destination emergences. I never considered writing a tell-all guide on when and where to go, with GPS coordinates of hotspots. It would have been an impossible task to list every waterway that hosts cicadas across the country. It would have also taken the fun out of trying something that can be a great experience with the right knowledge, understanding, and sense of adventure. Increased angling pressure, rising temperatures, lower snowpack, and loss of access impacts many of our favorite waterways. Certainly, conversation about epic fishing with big bugs on small waters has an impact. I urge the reader not only to sample some of these locations but also to research and hunt their own. It will be well worth your time and effort. Use this book as a resource to locate new opportunities and check for emergence on your local and destination waterways.

I selected the destinations for this book based on access, variety, and quality of fish and the ability of these waters to accommodate angling pressure. These areas not only

Picking apart a small western stream in early summer during cicada time

harbor excellent cicada fishing opportunities, but many of them are well known for their hatches and dry-fly fishing in earlier and later parts of the season. Read between the lines here, and recall that if one waterway hosts cicadas, nearby areas likely will as well. Enjoy the process of research. You just might find your new "secret spot."

TOP TO BOTTOM—THE YOUGHIOGHENY RIVER
Southwest Pennsylvania

The Youghiogheny, or "the Yough" (pronounced "Yock") as locals call it, is a river that crosses three state lines on its 134-mile journey toward Pittsburgh, Pennsylvania, as a tributary of the Monongahela River. The name "Youghiogheny" is roughly translated as "a stream flowing in a contrary direction" by Native Americans. This contrary direction is north, with its headwaters in Preston County, West Virginia, an area with no shortage of wilderness and steep hills, just on the border of Pennsylvania and Maryland.

Anyone intimate with the Yough will discuss the river divided into its major sections from "top to bottom." The "Top Yough" is the section of river in western Maryland beginning at Swallow Falls State Park downstream to Sang run. This is a 3.5-mile stretch of Class IV and V whitewater. The fishing in this section is primarily for trout and small-mouth bass, but obviously it is very difficult to navigate the river. Fishing on the edges and rock scrambling is possible but difficult. The big draw for this stretch is whitewater kayaking and recreational rafting.

The "Upper" is also an extremely popular stretch for recreational whitewater kayaking and rafting. This is approximately a 10-mile stretch from Sang run to Friendsville, Maryland. The excitement in this part of the river is largely due to the 115-feet-per-mile drop in the 5-mile-long canyon section. Releases from nearby Deep Creek supplement the flow here for rafters. Similar to the Top section, fishing is difficult for trout and bass

Steve Ludwig nets a Youghiogheny carp during annual cicadas.

here. But it is a wilderness setting, and few places more beautiful exist. The Deep Creek outflow is managed as a trout fishery and receives annual stockings.

As the river makes its way toward Pennsylvania, its flows are restricted to filling the valley ahead of the 184-foot dam near the town of Confluence, creating Yough Lake. The lake itself is an unrestricted motor class lake popular with water-skiers, Jet Skis and powerboating. Fishing can be good in the lake with large and smallmouth bass, walleye, carp and other warmwater fish. During 2016 Brood V cicadas, the lake brought these fish to the surface. Fishing from a boat in coves and along banks produced results.

Below the dam, the river becomes more of interest to fly anglers and conventional fishers alike. This is effectively the beginning of the 9-mile section known as the "Middle Yough" on its way to the mountain town of Ohiopyle. The dam operates as a bottom release, providing cool and clear water for the rest of the river year-round. In most summers, the Middle retains surface temperature in the 60s but can reach the low 70s farther downstream. The water in this section is big and harbors many Class I to III rapids, based on the water levels. It is tough wading, with a few spots that are accessible relatively easily. The Great Allegheny Passage (GAP) bike trail parallels the entire length of the river from the dam to its confluence with the Monongahela River on the southeastern edge of Pittsburgh. This trail is not only useful for access to harder-to-reach wade spots, but also as a convenient method to shuttle cars for float trips by bike.

At the dam site, there is a campground with bathrooms, showers, full hookups for RVs, and an improved boat ramp. The river here is wadable from either bank, though crossing the river is only possible in a few areas. Be careful wading here as it is slippery, swift, and cool, even in hot summertime temperatures. Just downstream from the dam is the town of Confluence, which is aptly named for the convergence of the Casselman, Laurel Hill Creek, and the Youghiogheny here. Laurel hill Creek meets the Casselman about 200 yards from where the Casselman meets the Youghiogheny. This area experiences a drastic temperature change in the convergence of the two rivers. Pay special attention to this while fishing in the area. Fish tend to congregate right at this confluence. I have seen northern pike in this area, and smallmouth bass stacked here during the fall.

The Casselman not only brings warmer water into the Youghiogheny, but also nutrients that help improve bug life in the Yough. Be aware, though, that the Casselman and Laurel Hill Creek muddy quickly after rainstorms, which can affect the clarity of the Yough significantly. At the beginning of a rain event, the river's right bank will be muddy, but the left bank will remain clear until the first set of rapids and the river-right bend at the Ramcat access. Here, the waters mix and tend to either dilute or blow out the remainder of the river.

At Ramcat, there is walk-in access for rafts, kayaks, and inflatables. Over the years, access has changed here, from being able to drive down with a trailer to being gated and walk-in only. This is a highly used area, and it is multiuse—bike trail, paddling, and recreational access as well as anglers. The outfitters out of Ohiopyle use this access to begin their Middle Yough trips. Please be respectful and understanding; everyone is there for a good time. This access is wadable in most areas and follows "trophy trout" regulations imposed by the Pennsylvania Fish and Boat Commission. While most anglers practice catch-and-release fishing for trout, the limit is one fish over 18 inches combined species, brown, rainbow, or brook trout. For wading anglers, use the bike trail to either walk or bike downstream from the Ramcat access to reach other areas that are less pressured. A short three-mile bike ride gets you to the island section, which is popular for wading and has plenty of room and access to prime sections full of trout.

A Youghiogheny brown trout caught near Ramcat

As the river makes its way downstream to Ohiopyle, it changes back to Class I–III whitewater sections with deep boulder fields. These areas are hard to wade but can be fished by hopping boulders. The river narrows and is deeper and wilder in some sections here, with long back eddies that funnel food and keep fish interested. Pay attention to these areas, and scout them before casting in hopes of finding a rising fish.

Where the Middle Yough shines is float fishing. The use of a raft or drift boat allows access and fishability to sections out of reach to wading anglers. Float trips on the Middle can be DIY or through guide services offered in Ohiopyle. Laurel Highlands Guide Service is the premier, longtime guide service on the river. The guides in this outfit have several lifetimes of experience on many of the river's sections, and many of the guides have spent their childhoods fishing the Yough. I highly recommend fishing with them as the best way to familiarize yourself with the river and techniques for success.

Anglers with a raft or drift boat can access the Middle at the improved trailer access at the campground entrance just below the dam. The take-out is at the Route 381 bridge in Ohiopyle. During summer months, don't plan on being alone—the river is a recreational hotspot, with the Middle Yough's mix of riffles, rapids, and slow sections a good mix for first-time or beginner recreational rafters, kayakers, and tubers, who frequent the river on weekends. Mid-week boat traffic is low to nonexistent. If intending to float the Middle, use caution, wear a life vest, and plan ahead. There are numerous online resources on navigating the rapids on all sections of the Yough. Always scout rapids, as river levels can change rapidly, and a rise or drop in water can significantly change the significance of danger at each rock or boulder in the river.

The fishing on the Middle is primarily trout and smallmouth bass. Each year, the Pennsylvania Fish and Boat Commission and several private clubs stock thousands of fingerlings and adult brown and rainbow trout in the river via float stocking. Many of these fish survive to reach their upper 20s in subsequent years. Every year a news article or two pops up with a photograph of an angler with a gangly, old hook-jawed brown trout pushing close to 30 inches. They are in there. Go find them. The smallmouth bass fishery can be excellent throughout this section, especially in the area around the confluence of the Casselman River as well as the slower, deep sections between riffles. This section has Brood V periodical cicadas, which bring the river's trout to the surface to feed. The next occurrence is 2033.

The town of Ohiopyle and the surrounding state park are a hidden gem in the Laurel Highlands. This small mountain and river town sits right in the middle of a recreational paradise. The town has a few longtime residents and many pioneers in the whitewater industry. Immersion Research, Wilderness Voyagers, and Airtight Inflatables all started here in support of the booming whitewater river running industry in the late 1970s and 1980s. The "shredder," an inflatable pontoon-style raft, was invented here and is a daily sight on the Lower Yough. The town itself overlooks Ohiopyle Falls—an 18-foot natural drop that effectively separates the Middle Yough from the Lower. In this section, the river changes its character; here it becomes Pennsylvania's premier recreational whitewater river, with an average gradient of 25 feet per mile. The river creates a unique geographical feature from the falls downstream about one mile: the Ferncliff Peninsula. From the falls, the river cuts west through a boulder-lined canyon and makes a wide loop toward the north, creating a peninsula of land that is narrower than it is long. This first section is affectionately called "the loop" and has 7 of the 14 named Class III–IV rapids on the Lower. Kayakers and light rafts put their craft in at the falls, run the loop and carry out, hiking up the hill and across the Ferncliff Peninsula to run the loop again and again, taking multiple rides on the natural amusement park ride the river provides. It is nearly a perfect design. No shuttle necessary!

Fishing this section is not for the faint of heart. Boulder-hopping on either side of the river is possible, but crossing the river is not an option. Wading is difficult to impossible in the sections surrounding the loop as the banks are steep and boulder strewn, and the water is swift, to say the least. Below the loop, the river has riffles and slower sections between the bigger and bolder rapids on its way to the Bruner Run take-out. Access on the river-right side of the river through the loop is possible by taking a short hike on Ferncliff Trail or above the loop take-out to the falls. Boulder-hopping this side of the river leads upstream to the falls, which can provide excellent fishing for trout and smallmouth bass. On the river-left side of the river, a short hike down Meadow Run, which enters just below the rafting put-in, can provide excellent fishing. Further access to the lower river is only available via the bike trail that parallels the river and crosses it in two locations. When I fish this section, I ride my bike to the Bruner Run take-out and below. Few anglers put in the effort to fish down this far due to access and a long bike ride. But it is well worth it for excellent trout and smallmouth bass fishing. Wading becomes a bit easier as the river levels out in gradient to about five feet per mile as it makes its way toward Connellsville.

If planning to float the Lower, note that it is for experienced paddlers only, those who are capable of navigating Class I–V rapids and versed in river rescue. Recommended river levels for fishing are 1.6 to 3 feet. The state park office manages access to this section and requires a timed entry launch permit as well as a shuttle token for the Bruner Run take-out. The take-out has only an upper parking area, and no private vehicles are allowed to drive to the lower lot. The state runs a shuttle service that will take you and your gear to the upper lot to retrieve your vehicle. Because of this, trailered boats are not allowed. Rafts, kayaks, and other self-carry inflatables are allowed as dictated by the take-out requirements. If planning to run this section, book a trip with one of the outfitters in town. They have experienced river guides who will navigate you safely through the numerous Class II–V whitewater rapids.

As the river makes its way downstream, another face of the Yough shows. The "Bottom" Yough, perhaps the longest section of the river, runs for the next 60 or so miles until its confluence with the Monongahela River, which converges with the Ohio River, meandering west to the Mississippi and then terminating in the Gulf of Mexico. Here, the river becomes an excellent bass and warmwater fishery. Several access points exist, with the bike trail continuing to provide access to every inch of the river. At Connellsville, an improved boat ramp is a popular start for drift boats, kayaks, and canoes, with multiple options for downstream take-outs in Dawson, Layton, Perryopolis, Whitsett, Cedar Creek Park, West Newton, and Sutersville. Most of these locations are popular with recreational tubers, and a number of shuttle and rental services can be easily accessed.

The author with a "Bottom" Yough carp on a cicada pattern

A solid Yough rainbow during Brood V. It will be several years before periodicals occur again on the river.

Cicadas on the Yough

Contributed by Mike Engelhardt

"If I go get my phone, will you eat another one on camera?" the kid said in a somewhat nervous, somewhat excited tone.

"Sure, they're not bad if you take the wings off first," I said, as I grabbed a freshly emerged cicada that happened to be crawling up my leg and removed the wings. He dashed away to get his phone and returned within seconds with the video already recording. Rest assured, if I ever run for public office (I won't), you'll surely see a video of a somewhat inebriated Mike chomping down a helpless, black-and-orange bug to the disgust of several of people around a fire ring somewhere along the Youghiogheny River.

In our defense, we had good reason to be acting a little foolish, and there are a lot worse things you can do on camera than washing down a crunchy little asparagus-flavored bug with a cold beer. The Brood V cicadas had been hiding under our feet for the last 17 years, and now it was time for them to become fish food on our home water: the roughly 70-mile section of the Youghiogheny (aka Yough) River from the town of Confluence to the Monongahela River in Elizabeth, Pennsylvania. A piece of water that is almost evenly split as a coldwater fishery and warmwater fishery. A "target rich environment" indeed.

Leading up to the emergence, guide calendars had a few more gaps left in them than normal, vacation days were scheduled by those with 9 to 5s, and enough flies were tied to fish the next 10 cicada emergences. The hunt for information was borderline obsessive. Stories were seined out of conversations with anglers who had been around for the last emergence to try to gain some intel, but returns were minimal. All we could seemingly turn up were stories such as, "The bugs never came off the hilltops. The fish had no idea what they were." Or, "The bugs were everywhere around the river, but the bass never really got on them. I gave up after a few tries and fished a Clouser Minnow. Caught a bunch that way."

We knew better. Previous experience fishing periodical cicada emergences had taught us that many anglers looked in the wrong places, or for the wrong species, or just didn't look hard enough before writing the whole experience off.

By mid-May, our usual floats had a few more stops built into them to check our favorite sections of river for dime-size holes in the ground and discarded cicada shells along our favorite runs. Cicada tracks, if you will.

The trill of cicadas began shortly after noticing the emergence tunnels, and it seemed as though the piles of exoskeletons split during each bug's emergence grew by the day. By the end of what turned out to be an abnormally hot May, sections of river had cicadas singing to the point of being almost deafening. We knew that this would be "the longest yard" from previous experiences fishing periodical cicadas. You see, cicadas are a terrestrial insect. Fish really don't recognize them as a food source until they've seen quite a few. Local weather, water clarity, and even nuances of individual fish species can cause this recognition period to take what seems to be an excruciating amount of time.

And then, one day, the switch just flipped:

- "Saw a group of six carp cruising like battleships pushing from bug to bug. There weren't many bugs, but the ones that were on the water didn't make it very far. Clumsy eats."
- "XYZ lake had wakes and lips poking up all over it when I drove by tonight. Might have saw some whiskers poking up too. Made a few casts from the bank and caught five before dark."
- "Floated the river today, wore this thing out (accompanied by a photo of what appeared to be a cicada pattern that was either taken to a belt sander after several shotgun blasts, or had a few too many encounters with some fat river rainbows)."

One of the well-fed rainbows on the Yough

In the week that followed, trout seemed to slash the bugs with reckless abandon when you could find a bank that had a bigger concentration of cicadas, but would seemingly ignore the big bugs in sections with riparian areas that were less populated with cicadas. Initially many rises to the big bug were misses, almost as if the trout didn't know how to eat after a spring of sipping bugs that seemed tiny in comparison to a big cheeseburger-like bug. As the emergence continued on, more and more bugs hit the water and the trout grew very comfortable sucking them down. By mid-June, a cicada that ended up in the cold water of the "Middle" or "Lower" Yough had a good chance of meeting its end in the jaws of an opportunistic, and often rather large, lumpy-bellied salmonid.

When it came to the healthy population of smallmouth bass that reside in the Yough from top to bottom, we regrettably found that the old-timer's tip of fishing a Clouser Minnow during the last emergence was spot on. Any angler that has pursued smallmouth knows that they are more than willing to eat bugs off the surface (including the annual "dog day" cicadas). Naturally, one would think that inundating the river with a bunch of twitching, strong-silhouetted, high-protein morsels on a warm June day would make for some pretty memorable topwater fishing, but that wasn't the case. Plenty of time was spent speculating as to why the bass fishing with cicadas wasn't on par with the other species, but in the interest of complete candor, we kind of didn't care. We really aren't fans of fishing smallmouth during and in the period immediately following the spawn, and as the saying goes, there were bigger fish to fry.

Those bigger fish came in the form of a large-bodied, rubber-lipped member of the minnow family: the common carp. Thanks to their intelligence, ability to exist (if not thrive) just about anywhere, and willingness to test your backing knots, carp have been doing a pretty good job of shaking off the "trash fish" label and earning some serious respect as a worthy fly rod target. The Brood V emergence only strengthened the case for that respect by highlighting their willingness to feed on the surface.

Having a great hatch on some of your favorite water is a pretty good recipe for making some memories, and we certainly filled the memory banks with plenty of images of trout acting fool-ish during the Brood V emergence, but the most vivid memories will always be tied to chasing carp. Sure, big browns and rainbows exploding on dry flies is fun, but when you compare it with watching a 10-plus-pound carp cruising a big river eddy with his equally large buddies that are *actively hunting* for bugs and having the guys in the boat feed those fish on the surface, there's not even a comparison. The whole scenario is visual and physically demanding from start to fin-ish, and what self-respecting fly angler wouldn't love that?

After a few days of chasing river carp, we were set on a great program. Float down the river while both anglers and the oarsman look for nervous water, wakes, or even orange lips poking up in eddies, under trees, or on wide-open flats. Much like being on the bow of a flats skiff, both anglers peeled a workable length of line off their reels and held the fly in their hand ready to be delivered on the double to a cruising carp. The carp weren't the only ones that were hunting on the river.

"There he is. About one o'clock. About 40 feet in front. Under that silver maple. See him?" my good friend Josh Reffner said calmly as he was already one false cast into delivering the fly to the fish that I hadn't even seen yet from the rower's bench. Josh is an accomplished angler and hunter, and his "hunter's vision" was showing itself daily on the river. The ice water that seemingly flows through his veins after years of intense hunting situations was becoming more and more apparent with each carp interaction as well. I'm not a hunter, but I understand that having the ability to take a "shot" when it presented itself, or letting a situation play out so that a shot presents itself is integral to being successful. In this particular case, the scenario required both attributes to be used at nearly the same time.

On the second false cast, Josh dropped the fly in the sunlit piece of water just upriver from the shade of the overhanging maple that was leaning over the water so hard that it only offered about two feet of clearance between the water's surface and the lowest-hanging branches of the tree. We had a front-row seat, and the show was about to start. As the fly drifted into the shade line, I saw the water bulge and a rather large set of orange lips broke the surface. "Got him!" I said, but there was no reaction from the front of the boat. Josh just stared where the fly was and didn't say a word.

You see, the downturned, rubbery mouth of a carp isn't exactly built for feeding on the surface, and trying to suck in a big chunk of foam only exaggerates this design flaw. We had already seen several carp seemingly miss or lose the fly when they looked to be locked in to eat it, and learned that a quick hookset was an almost surefire way to blow a golden opportunity. We even modified fly patterns to ride lower in the water and have more mass to avoid being pushed away from the clumsy carp eats.

Much like a buzzer-beater shot at the end of a basketball game that goes around the hoop a few times before dropping into the net, Josh's fly was bouncing around the lips of the carp that was determined to eat it. The fly bounced off those big orange lips over and over again as they opened and closed, trying desperately to find the fly by feel. Obviously, this happened over the course of a few seconds, but from my vantage point, it seemed like an eternity.

Finally, on what seemed like the 10th try, the carp sucked the whole bug in, and the lips went back under the surface. It was at that point I finally heard the sound that every angler loves to hear—that distinct sound of fly line ripping off the water and coming tight to an angry fish.

I looked over to Josh, who was grinning ear to ear while doing a little tap dance to make sure the remaining line was clear of his feet as the carp sped downriver trying to get away from whatever conundrum he had just gotten himself into. Josh's reel was screaming, and in a matter of moments, the backing knot ticked its way through the guides. This was a bigger class of fish than the others we had grown comfortable with, both in terms of size and attitude. He was now into the backing and zigzagging back and forth across the river. As carp often do, the fish seemed to know where each snag was that could help him shake loose from the fly and was doing his best to find a stick, boulder, or rotted-out lawnmower carcass (we were carp fishing after all) that was anchored in the river bottom waiting to wrap Josh's line and break free.

An 8-weight, 0x tippet and a heavy-gauge hook gave Josh the leverage he needed to steer the fish clear and into a boat net that normally feels oversized, but this time felt a little small for its new guest. In short order, photos were snapped, carp slime high fives were exchanged, and fresh celebratory beers were cracked. We knew what just happened was certainly going to be a high point of this emergence, but there wasn't much time to soak it all in. A pair of wakes downriver reminded us that it was time to get back to the game. After all, the Brood V hourglass was getting low on sand, and we would have 17 more years to replay and celebrate the good times after we educated a few more of those slimy carp. ●

Mike Engelhardt with a battleship of a carp. MIKE ENGELHARDT

Fishing this section can be excellent, especially during periodical and annual cicada emergences. During 2016, Brood V periodicals emerged on the entire 74 miles of river in Pennsylvania. The bottom sections fished particularly well for carp during the peak in the middle of June. I witnessed this emergence in 1999 and 2016 on the Bottom Yough and made several return trips for carp and a few catfish that hunted cicadas.

In mid- to late summer, pay attention to the annual cicadas on the Bottom Yough. Late July and August bring the return of several species of large *Neotibicen* cicadas that sing along the banks of the hottest days of summer. There are a moderate number of these bugs on the entire lower river, and bass anglers should take note. As mentioned previously, dead drifting a large, black or olive deer hair, foam-, or cork-bodied fly under overhanging trees can result in the best fish of the year. This fishing sometimes continues through September. A tactic on this section of river is to float the river with two anglers. The front angler floats a dead-drifted bug on the bank in front of the boat, and the rear angler fishes out of the back of the boat with a baitfish or crayfish pattern. This allows "full coverage" top to bottom, to key on bass as baitfish, crayfish, or cicada chasers, which bass at this time of year can't seem to get enough of.

The Youghiogheny holds a special place in the heart of many anglers. The opportunities and variety in water type, species, and scenery that it affords makes it worth a visit.

THE PENNSYLVANIA TRIO OF TROUT STREAMS
A Love Letter to Central Pennsylvania

Pennsylvania is home to a long line of well-known and famous fly anglers, guides, and fly tiers. George Harvey, Joe Humphreys, Vince Maranaro, Ed Shenk, Charlie Meck, Charlie Fox, Bob Clouser, George Daniel, and several others call Pennsylvania their home. It is no coincidence either; volumes of works have been written about Pennsylvania's trout,

A Spring Creek brown trout caught on a Hippie Stomper dressed like a cicada pattern

streams, and hatches. Probably the most storied waters are those located in the central part of the state, namely Centre County, the home of Penn State University. There is more water here than one can fish and master in several lifetimes.

The heart of Centre County is called "Happy Valley," with the origin of its nickname dating back to the 1930s, during the Great Depression. Because of the state university, this area was not financially hit as hard as other surrounding areas. My sentiments for this area, and personal definition of "Happy Valley," is a little different today, as the valley is synonymous with dry flies and wild rising trout to me. I'm sure other fly anglers feel the same way. The area is full of options, many within a short drive of each other.

I include these creeks because not only do they provide year-round quality fly fishing for wild trout, but they are all in the geographic location of Brood XIV, last emerging in 2008 and returning in 2025.

Spring Creek

Situated minutes outside State College Pennsylvania and flowing right through the town of Bellefonte, Spring Creek is perhaps one of the most accessible, wadable, and prolific wild trout streams in the state. The area's geography, geology, and tributaries contribute to why this stream is as good as it is. Spring Creek is relatively short—only 22 miles from source to confluence. At the source, its headwaters begin near Boalsburg, a small town near Tussey Mountain, emerging from limestone formations that provide cold, clear water with high alkalinity. On its way toward State College, it picks up key high-quality tributaries that further add to its flow. Slab Cabin Run, Cedar Run, Logan Branch, Buffalo Run, and several unnamed spring tributaries are all small, brushy wild trout streams that converge with Spring Creek and provide consistent cold water that keeps the main creek cool all summer long.

The state provides several access points along its length, near the Benner Run Fish Hatchery and at Fisherman's Paradise and Tallyrand Park in the town of Bellefonte. Perhaps the best known of these is Fisherman's Paradise, located just above Bellefonte off Route 550. This area has a history of fly fishing in a parklike setting dating back to the 1930s. It has been managed as "heritage angling" for as long as I can remember fishing it—no wading and barbless flies only. The trout in this section are highly educated and hip to the latest and greatest fly patterns year-round. In fact, it is said that somewhere on Spring Creek trout rise 365 days per year, and I believe it. I would put my money down on the Paradise section.

For perhaps the best fishing on the creek, it's a toss-up between the sections above and below the Paradise. Above the Paradise is a walk-in section with an access road paralleling the creek most of the way. If you are willing to walk, you can find some solitude, but use the number of cars in the parking lot as your gauge. A lot of anglers take this walk and fish the upper water.

Below the Paradise, the "cottage section" continues to the bridge crossing at Route 550. This section is perhaps my favorite, despite being directly roadside, but it really is all good water. The creek opens up here and is classic riffle-pool water, perfect for mayflies and dry-fly fishing. Landowners in this section are used to anglers; nonetheless, always be respectful and thank them for the access. Pick up trash and leave only footprints. Below Route 550, the creek has two major springs that further increase the creek's flow as it makes its way through Bellefonte and to the confluence with Bald Eagle Creek—a great trout fishing creek as well. Spring Creek is accessible for most of its length here, with only a few places of posted property preventing access.

Over the years, Spring Creek has been plagued by problems—typical problems of being located in a fast-growing area, increased development, sedimentation, runoff, loss of riparian buffers, depleting aquifers, and reckless industrial accidents. Some work has been done to reverse this, as the creek has many supporters and proponents. The McCoy-Linn Dam removal of 2007 was one of these, and illustrated just how fast a creek can bounce back. This dam was approximately 12 feet high, backing up flow between Bellefonte and Milesburg, just above Spring Creek's confluence with Bald Eagle Creek. There have been various dams at this site since the 1700s, mainly for industrial water supply in the early steel industry in Pennsylvania and later as hydropower. Defunct since the 1950s, the dam served no purpose. In 2007 it was removed, and the stream channel was restored and stabilized. The first time I fished this section was barely a year after the dam's removal in 2008, during the emergence of Brood XIV. It was back, and it was good! Fish moved into the new habitat, bug life was present, and water quality to the lower river was improved, providing Bald Eagle with cold water and improved fishing as well.

Brood XIV emerged in June of 2008 throughout Spring Creek's entire 22-mile drainage. That season was blessed with significant spring rain, filling underground aquifers and providing cold water through the peak of the emergence in mid-June. This was incredible fishing, with trout looking up for cicadas for almost an entire month.

Penns Creek

Mention Penns Creek to a dry-fly angler and they will likely share a memory or experience about the famous Green Drake hatch the river experiences in late May, usually around Memorial Day weekend. The Drakes are legendary, predictable, and really something to experience. Penns is a gorgeous trout stream in a wilderness setting with equally gorgeous wild trout.

Penns Creek is a long, free-running limestone stream of medium to large size that emerges from the ground at Penns Cave near the town of Centre Hall. The cave itself is an attraction, with tours by boat offering a close look at the limestone formations that contribute to the water quality of the creeks in this region. From its emergence at the cave, Penns works its way easterly through the town of Spring Grove, an area that is primarily agricultural, on its way to Coburn. Because of the agriculture in this area, Penns warms quickly, suffers from sediment, and is temperamental during rainstorms. Even short, but heavy downpours can lead to blowout and chocolate milk for days.

At the town of Coburn, a major tributary, Elk Creek, enters Penns and rejuvenates its cold flows. The start of the "All-Tackle Trophy" trout area begins at the confluence and extends for about seven miles to the campground at Poe Paddy. Central to this section is Ingleby, which I wouldn't say is necessarily a "town," but it is a place to park and access the stream's best sections. I like to park in this section and walk the trail either up- or downstream to find rising fish in the numerous pools in the area.

From Poe Paddy downstream approximately four miles to Cherry Run is the catch-and-release section. This section gets a lot of attention, especially during the Drakes.

In 2008, Brood XIV also emerged in the valley of Penns Creek. Emergence of this brood began in early June, with the peak number of flying and mating bugs around the summer solstice, June 20. Air temperatures were prime for cicadas—in the mid-80s—but poor for trout. We elected to not fish Penns Creek as water temperatures were dangerous and rising in the following weeks. Please follow suit when targeting trout during the summer months; carry a thermometer and focus on cooler streams, chase warmwater species, or don't fish!

The Little Juniata River

The story of the Little Juniata River is a story of comeback. The "Little J" or "J," as most of us and locals refer to it, was not always what it looks like today. Drive along its banks in the spring and you will see a beautiful river with a chalky-green tint as it winds through tight canyons, lined with hardwoods and the pink flowers of redbuds on the hillsides. Even the numerous hand-cut stone-arched railroad bridges are a sight to behold. Look a little closer and you might see a trout rise to a mayfly or caddis.

It wasn't always this way.

In the 1960s and 1970s, the river was devoid of trout and insects, but full of industrial and residential waste. Cleanup efforts and infrastructure improvements on the federal and local level have transformed this river from a sewer ditch into a world-class, multiuse trout stream that continues to get better with each passing season.

The J begins as a small stream that converges with several named and unnamed tributaries as it winds northeast through the Logan Valley near Altoona, Pennsylvania, for 35 miles on its way to join its larger sibling, the Juniata River. Fishing through the Altoona area is a mix of stocked and wild fish in a semi-urban town setting. The river gets warm here as it winds through the valley, but that changes quickly at Tyrone. There, the river cuts east through limestone outcroppings and steep hills where it picks up several springs, improving the water quality and dropping the temperature. The springs are abundant; you can feel the temperature fluctuations when wet wading in early summer. This section hardly has a bad spot on its way to its confluence with Spruce Creek. It is

A typical brown trout on the Little Juniata River

incredibly perfect trout water, alternating between riffles and pools for several miles. The river is wadable in most sections, although river crossings are possible only in a few areas. The fish here are numerous and can grow large due to the cover, depth, and availability of food the river provides. Hatches are prolific, with Blue-Winged Olives, Grannoms, Sulphurs, and March Browns providing dry-fly action from March to June. Aside from periodical cicada emergences, don't wait to fish the J; the Sulphur hatches in May are really something to experience, with huge numbers of bugs, massive spinner falls at dusk, and incredible numbers of rising trout.

From Spruce Creek to Barree, access is limited but available for those who want to walk. Parking is available at the town of Spruce Creek at roadside pull-offs, and the Spruce Creek United Methodist Church located at the bridge over the river near the confluence of the Little Juniata and Spruce Creek, which allows angler parking apart from church service times. Be respectful to church patrons and their property. This is a major multiuse access point for anglers, kayakers, and tubers in the summer. Pick up trash and say thanks. At Barree, there are pull-offs and a Rothrock State Forest trail parking area. It gets crowded here, but you can easily walk between the two areas. On the upper end, a private club from Spruce Creek downstream for about a mile occupies the river left bank, while the river right bank is impassable and posted. You can walk this section; however, you must remain within the high-water mark. The J is deemed "navigable," which means the river bottom cannot be owned in Pennsylvania. The club owns the land, not the river. Be respectful, follow the rules, and enjoy.

Below Barree, the river is joined by the Frankstown Branch of the Little Juniata River near Petersburg and gains appreciable size and flow, and increased temperature, as it makes its way to join the Juniata River. Trout fishing continues throughout the river system.

The 2008 emergence of Brood XIV also occurred here in epic proportions. The river between Tyrone and Barree remained cold, clear, and fishable, the cicadas were prolific, and I caught some of my most memorable trout that year on the river. It takes a lot for large brown trout to feed on the surface in bright sunlight. During the peak of cicada flying activity, trout could be seen hunting for the insects in many of the flat pools on the river. It seemed that almost any drift—dragging or not—through fast water would produce a strike. The fishing continued to be good through the end of June and beyond the Fourth of July that year.

FISHING IN THE AQUARIUM: THE GREEN RIVER

The Green River, situated in the northeast corner of Utah, is one of those places that when you take your first drift boat ride through the canyon, you have no idea where to look. Do you look at the trout swimming for cover under the boat in the gin-clear water, or the morning sun reflecting off the red stone cliffs, or the eagle flying overhead, or . . . hey look! Petroglyphs!

John Wesley Powell visited the Green and Colorado Rivers in 1869. He described the canyon as a "flaring, brilliant red gorge." One visit to the area and you will quickly see he wasn't wrong. Flaming Gorge Dam, completed in 1964, holds back almost 4 million gallons of water, most of which sits in Wyoming. This dam, in addition to dams on the Colorado River, were created as part of the Bureau of Reclamation's Colorado River Storage Project, spawned from an earlier agreement, the 1922 Colorado River Basin Compact. This divided the land along the Colorado River into two basins: Utah, Colorado, and Wyoming in one basin and California, Arizona, and Nevada in the other.

Colby Crossland's brown trout–themed drift boat against the red cliffs of the A section on the Green River. The beauty of the canyon encompasses not only what's beneath the surface, but above it too.

This agreement drafted the initial allotment of water to each basin, further divided up by the individual states. With western sprawl and urban development, there was increasing yearly water usage in the basin containing California, directly impacting water availability in the other basin. In 1956, the Colorado River Storage Project was passed by Congress and directly funded the creation of Flaming Gorge Dam.

The dam, approximately 450 feet above the Green River, sits adjacent to the town of Dutch John, a one-light town complete with three fly shops, a shuttle service, a campground, and a convenient store. It's a trout town if I ever saw one. Dutch John didn't exist before the first concrete was poured at the dam site; it was originally a federally funded town set up for the workers who built Flaming Gorge Dam. It certainly looks that way as well, with single-story, slab-construction, cookie-cutter houses lining the short streets in town. The town has a special charm these days—with the majority of houses remodeled, complete with drift boats or rafts on trailers parked in the driveway.

In terms of a trout river, the Green River below the dam is relatively new. Previous to the dam, the river was a tepid, silty stream home to members of the pikeminnow family and not much else, typical of desert rivers and streams. With the filling of the reservoir and the newly installed dam, the river now spilling through the drain of a nearly 500-foot-deep reservoir was clear—no longer silty, and no longer warm. The installation of the dam created a near-perfect environment for trout. Bottom release gates in the dam enabled clear, cold water releases to combat high summer temperatures as well as increased light, which resulted in increased macroinvertebrate development leading to a high biomass. Trout were introduced and almost immediately thrived. Browns dominate the fishery, though no additional browns are stocked today. It is a self-sustaining population of wild fish from those initial stockings. The rainbows that populate the river are a result of yearly plantings of year-old hatchery fish. Some of these fish reach adult age and can grow very large; however, it is believed that rainbows only exist as a result of the seasonal stockings. A theory as to why this is the case has to do with the spawning times for each species. Browns naturally spawn in the fall and rainbows in the spring. Egg survival is great for the brown trout because in the fall, stable flows govern the river. In the spring, flows are often higher with runoff and regulated periods to enable the native fish, members of the pikeminnow family, to have their chance at spawning in silty, fast water. This coincides with rainbow and cutthroat trout spawning seasons, and it is thought that the higher flows wipe out any spawning habitat and significantly reduce trout egg survival.

Nonetheless, there are plenty of trout in the Green. So many, in fact, that the first several miles of the river below the dam are sometimes called "the aquarium." Surveys over the years have resulted in numbers fluctuating from 8,000 to 14,000 trout per mile. It is absolutely incredible to float through some sections and see dozens, sometimes hundreds, of trout in plain view. With that many targets, opportunities to catch fish are very high. Because of the ability for a long growing season, predictable flows and temperatures, and food availability, the average fish is between 16 and 18 inches. Many larger fish exist. I have heard stories and seen photographs of fish near 30 inches—caught on dry flies. Yep.

The river is divided into several sections, notably A, B, and C starting from the dam to some 40 miles to one of the many take-outs on the C section. The A section is a must-do, if nothing else, to see the sights and learn about the canyon and its history. I had the pleasure to spend two days with Colby Crossland, a guide for Spinnerfall Guide Service, fishing out of his brown trout–themed drift boat. Colby shared the names of rapids, trees, birds, and even rocks along our trip. During the first few minutes of our float, I may have had to apologize for the lack of conversation, as I was enamored with everything around me. On our drive to the ramp at the base of the dam, Colby asked us what we wanted to do for the day's trip. I was quick to answer, "Dry flies and cicadas, I don't care to streamer fish or watch bobbers." He smiled and said, "Oh, we're gonna have fun today."

We floated through both the A and B sections, with Colby rowing us way ahead in the morning, working hard to keep us in the lines on the river to drift our cicada patterns cleanly, and often to sight-fish the giant eddies after the numerous Class I–III rapids. We never were passed by another drift boat all day. I believe that our cicada patterns, the smaller *Platypedia putnami*, or Putnam's cicada—better yet "clicker" cicadas, as guides call them—were the first fakes the trout on the river saw that day. We caught fish, *a lot* of fish and some of them very big, on the black-and-orange foam flies.

We had a repeat performance on the A section again the following day; however, we opted to wade-fish a lot of the fast water once we drifted through. Our reasoning was that the fast water held a lot of fish tight to the banks. In a drift boat, the oarsman is doing his best to hold the boat in the current, but also must make moves to navigate the river safely. You might get one fish, or a refusal in this water, but certainly there are a lot more as you are whizzing by in the current, with the rower making moves to safely negotiate the section. Colby once again worked his shoulders off, eddying out at the end of rapids, dropping me off on one side of the river with a net and Bob Bell on the other to work both sides, up the bank, wet wading, drifting the big bugs, and hooking several fish each.

The beauty of the Green—both above and below the water—is exceptional. Visit once and you will make plans to visit again. Throw cicadas into that mix on a yearly basis, and it is a special opportunity to catch a ton of fish, some very big, on 2X tippet and #8–2 dry flies. It gets even better. Every year, the small *Platypedia* cicada happens on the river. On special years, two emergences occur and sometimes overlap. The *Okanagana magnifica* (guides call them mondos) can also make an appearance, which extends the cicada fishing almost a month. In other years, the giant shell-backed cricket, otherwise known as the Mormon cricket, can occur in biblical plague proportions. All of these occur on the riverbanks, which is a sure bet trout will be looking for them.

I walked the banks during our streamside lunches, looking for signs of emergence and making observations on habitat. Emergence holes were present on the banks, directly below many of the box elder and juniper trees. This is fairly low-canopy vegetation, but about the tallest tree species in most areas. Scrub, grasses, and some lodgepole pines also inhabit the riverbanks, and all had signs of emergence, from holes at the bases of trees and vegetation to nymphal shucks still clinging to tree bark.

I missed the emergence of the mondos and the Mormon crickets that followed. But I did not feel the same FOMO that I normally do when a buddy sends photos of the fish they caught while I'm facing a computer screen on the job. I arguably experienced the best of the "clickers," as we were right on the front edge of the fish that were looking for them and not yet picky with imitations. It's possibly a blessing that we missed the Mormon crickets, as those things bite!

At the time of this writing, the states that receive water in the Colorado River drainage are facing an uncertain future. A ten-year drought, reduced snowpack, and reservoirs at all-time lows have caused states to ration not only water, but electricity, too. The dams also create hydroelectric power, and with rationing of water comes the reality of insufficient electricity production. Brownouts, blackouts, and mandatory blackout periods

Cicadas on the Green

Contributed by Colby Crossland

Clickers/minis, buzzers/mondos, yellow-bellies—the Green has a plethora of cicadas that reside in the hills and mountains that surround it. Throw in hoppers, a few golden stones, and the random herd of Mormon crickets and you have one of the best big bug dry-fly rivers in the world. It was even where the foam fly originated in the 1990s, the birth of the Chernobyl Ant. The tough part is that as guides and fishers of the river, we know very little about our big bugs.

We have annual cicadas, which we refer to as clickers or minis, that show up nearly every year. The year-to-year numbers of the hatch very greatly though, as do locations where they hatch. Some years there are only a few bugs, not worth trying to imitate on the river. One bug on the water does not make a hatch! On occasion, the cicadas will emerge in heavy numbers in very small stretches of the river. This may be a mile where they are thick and then completely absent on the rest of the river. Other years we have so many cicadas clicking, flying, and dropping onto the water that I have had clients catch fish on their backcasts. During these times, you can look downriver and see dozens of cicadas on the water, riverbank to riverbank. Most years fall somewhere in between. When they emerge is even a bit of a mystery too. It feels like we start seeing them ten warm, dry days after the first good rain in the spring. The first week of April, stories start being shared down "guide row" about someone finding one on the water. Very soon after the first reports, you'll see a couple photos hit Instagram with #cicada. After this initial burst of early emergers, we may not see any more for almost a month. It is usually around the middle to the end of May when we start seeing them in numbers high enough to truly get excited about, following the same pattern of heavy rain followed by a week or so of dry, warm temperatures. If the conditions do not match what the cicadas need to trigger emergence, they simply don't show up in fishable numbers and the mystery persists.

The early cicadas in the area are unique in their mating call. Instead of the typical droning buzz that most cicadas make, the small cicadas "click." The sound is a short burst of snappy sharp clicks. The cicadas that make this sound are mostly a dark gray color with pale orange legs and outer wing veins, not nearly as colorful as the orange used on most commercial patterns. In addition to calling them "clickers," we also call them "minis." They range in size #8–12 with a pretty narrow taper, no larger than a pencil and often smaller.

About a month after the minis, the much larger cicada may make an appearance. These are giant bugs, with imitations tied on a large, heavy hook. Because of their size, we call them "mondos." We also call them "buzzers" for the way they sound. The mondo's call is closer to what most people expect when thinking of cicadas—it is more of a loud humming drone.

On the river, we do not count on seeing the mondos nearly as often as the minis. It seems like we see them in fishable numbers about every four to five years. They are almost twice as long as the minis and quite a bit wider and squatter in appearance, like the butt of a smoked cigar! The thorax extends much farther down the body, with a short abdomen. The size of commercial flies will vary greatly in relation to the taper of the body. A size 6 is usually about right. For coloration they have much more contrast: black and gray, orange wing veins, and orange-striped abdomens. ●

A brown trout from the Green River

continue to occur across the western drainage of the mighty Colorado. When I visited the area in early June 2022, Flaming Gorge Reservoir was already down several feet, with an adjusted release schedule to provide more water downriver. The entire drainage of the Colorado River, including the Green River, faces an uncertain future in this age of climate change.

A philosophical debate may exist here regarding utilization of the resource, which was originally held back for water rationing, western development, and hydroelectric production, but inadvertently created an additional recreational industry with the manufactured trout fishery that is the lower Green we know today. We as fly anglers sometimes want to have our cake and eat it too—dams are bad for anadromous steelhead, but good for trout in desert landscapes like the Green, San Juan, and Colorado at Lees Ferry. But the fact is, these fisheries exist today, and the fish and cicadas on the Green offer one of the most unique and exciting experiences for a dry-fly cicada chaser.

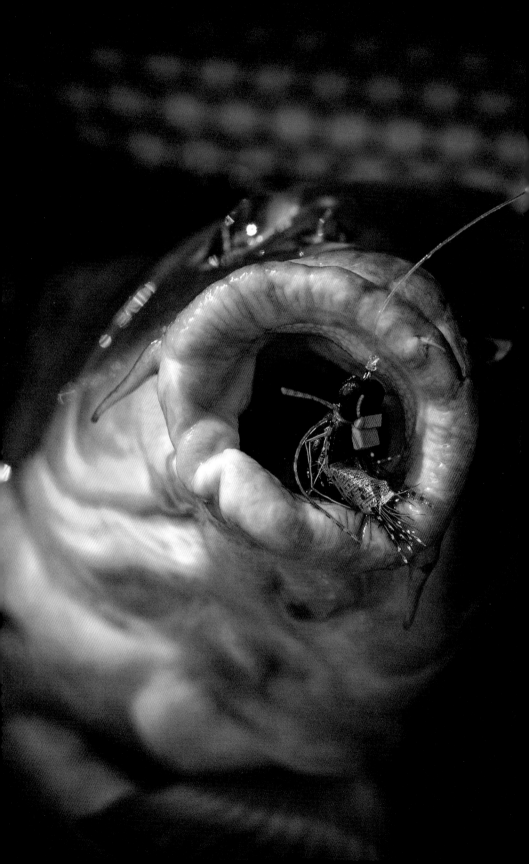

Cicada Imitations

THE PATTERNS INCLUDED IN THIS BOOK ARE VARIATIONS ON THE THEME of foam, natural fibers, and synthetic wing and leg materials borrowing from grasshopper, cricket, and beetle patterns. Chernobyl Ants, Dave's Hopper, and the multitude of foam hopper variations can all be adapted to match cicadas with tweaks to color and size. The three key ingredients to a successful pattern are 1) visibility to the angler, 2) wide body profile when viewed from below that sits low in the film, and 3) wings. In terms of wings, there are two basic profiles: wings that are in the folded or closed position, and wings that are splayed out. From the fish-eye view, they see a silhouette of size and shape. I go for this before moving on to match color and add details like eyes and segmentation. It makes sense to match the color and simulate transparent wings; after all, we are trying to match the hatch!

There are a few exceptions, however. Trout being trout, often perceived as picky or pressured, will sometimes inspect, bump, and "taste" flies before committing to eating. I have experienced carp feel a fly with their lips and closed mouth, then completely blow up away from the fly when they felt something was not right. The natural cicada is a hard-shelled insect with transparent, stiff, and crinkly wings and firm legs. I believe fish that have been stung repeatedly develop their senses to feel and can distinguish between

An army of periodical cicada imitations tied by the author in preparation for the 2019 Brood VIII emergence

A Chuck Kraft–style cicada imitation catches fish. Jimmy Guerrerio is all smiles when carp are looking up. Carry multiple patterns and various sizes for success. MIKE ENGELHARDT

real and fake. In cases like these, opting for stiffer wing and leg materials on patterns that are true to size and color may be necessary for success. Use deer hair and moose body and mane fibers to replicate stiffness, and use foams, rubber, and synthetic fibers to add softness to patterns. The patterns in this book range from simple and suggestive to realistic in size, profile, and coloration of the real thing. It never hurts to have a few patterns of each to match your fishing situations. It can be the difference between getting blanked or not!

In periodical emergences, very often you will encounter three species of cicadas, varying in size and color. During Brood X in 2021, we fished the northern end of a large lake that had almost solely *Magicicada septendecim*. The insects were nearly 1½ inches in length with an abdomen more orange than black, best imitated with an imitation in size 4 or 2. As we motored our boat to the southern end, we found the abundant species there was *M. cassini*, which were half the size with completely black bodies. We started to see refusals from fish on our much larger imitations. We had a few smaller variations on hand and trimmed our larger patterns to match the naturals. It was a good lesson in stocking your fly box with variations in size and color. Often, trying a smaller pattern will trigger a strike when getting refusals from larger patterns, even if the larger pattern is closer to the real thing.

The pattern, Dave's 17-Year Itch Cicada, is my go-to pattern for periodical cicada emergences, but has also proven successful on annual dog day cicadas when matched in size to the naturals present and in colors of olive, brown, and black. The pattern has been proven to be effective, durable, and quick to tie. When I developed this pattern, I wanted a durable fly that floated without the use of silicone or fly floatant, a segmented body that sat in the film, and a strong hook to resist bending or breaking from extended fights with 20-pound carp.

I based this pattern on the "Hopper Juan" tied by Colorado fly-fishing guide and tier Juan Ramirez. My pattern utilizes a similar approach in creating the two-piece foam segmented body. It also lends itself to wing variations, allowing the tier to mimic folded-wing, spent-wing, or fluttering styles. The basic pattern utilizes mostly synthetic materials, except for the standard elk hair wing. The pattern reliably lands in the upright position, and because of the use of thin craft foam, it floats but sits nicely in the film. Substitute open-cell fly foam for the top piece if you desire high-riding patterns. For an even lower pattern that sits just below the film, use Furry Foam, a popular material for making crayfish patterns, also used on George Daniel's sinking cicada pattern. The use of adhesive enables the fly to be extremely durable, and typically will hold up to many fish. I prefer the Gamakatsu B10S hook for patterns size 4 and up, as it is a strong, light, and fine wire hook with a micro-barb that can be pinched easily. This hook is known for heavy saltwater use and will hold up to the largest of freshwater gamefish. I invite you to tie a few, and try your own variations on the basic pattern in size, color, and wing materials for your next outing with cicadas!

Dave's 17-Year Itch Cicada pattern at the vise

Making Durable and Adaptable Patterns

Adhesives

A common material across any cicada pattern is the use of glue. Most of the patterns here use some sort of foam or fiber that requires glue to add to the durability of the finished fly. Cicada patterns are bulky and often possess a wide body profile and, when paired with a comparatively thin wired hook, have a tendency to spin on the shank. You want to avoid this on larger hook sizes as it will impede a proper hookup on trophy-size fish. In June 2022, I handed Colby Crossland one of my small cicada patterns that matched the cicadas along the riverbanks, and the first thing he did to the newly tied fly was check to see if the hook spun on the shank. The hook twisted, and he proceeded to repair my fly with superglue kept in his stash of guide tools, tricks, and tips. Guides see more flies than the fish do, and only after his repair did my pattern pass the test. I had used an old bottle of superglue when tying flies for that trip and the quality must have degraded (that's my story and I'm sticking to it!). Use fresh glue! Applying an adhesive along the hook shank when tying in new materials at each step is recommended.

Common glues typically used can range from cyanoacrylate types (commonly referred to as superglue or CA glue) to UV cure resins, rubber cement, and silicone types. I prefer to use Zap-A-Gap as a CA glue when tying foam imitations, and for adding durability and stiffness to the bodies of flies. For adhering eyes, legs, and rubber materials, E6000 or Goop is an excellent choice. Both are typically available at any hardware or big-box store. To keep your CA glue types fresh, refrigerate them and limit the amount of time the cap is off, as CA glue cures through water absorption in the form of humidity. Once opened, a bottle of CA glue is good for about a month or less.

Modern UV cure glues are also an excellent choice when the area to be glued can be exposed to light. These are special resins that harden when exposed to ultraviolet rays. Because these glues degrade and age once the bottle is opened, some of them never fully cure and can result in sticky flies. Setting completed bugs on a windowsill in the sun can help remedy longer cure times and sticky flies. Avoid using UV cure glues when you need to join two dark materials like pieces of foam, as the light energy cannot penetrate to cure the adhesive.

Rubber cement or contact cement, found in craft stores, can be an excellent choice for laminating foam to make bodies and popper heads. They are hard to use while constructing a fly, but easily used on raw materials like foam sheets to mass-produce variegated bodies such as Micah's Cicada and the Flip Flop Cicada.

Markers

Recently I started to carry a small range of permanent markers to adjust flies while on the water. Originally, I started doing this with streamer patterns that imitate baitfish. I tied them in pearl, white, or light gray then added contrast colors with permanent markers to create a darker backs, spots, or gills. This proved especially effective when fishing new waters and matching the local baitfish patterns, especially on saltwater beaches. Pinfish, whitebait, and emerald baitfish all vary in color, some with stripes and some without. By carrying generic patterns and being able to color them appropriately allowed for simplification both at the vise and in the fly box. The same holds true for cicada patterns, especially with annual species. Many are black, brown, amber, olive, and tan from the fish-eye view. By tying the underside a lighter hue, such as tan, white, or olive, you can adjust the color on the water with a few slashes of a permanent marker. I don't think it is ultra-critical to achieve perfection, but too light or too dark can make a difference to a selective fish. ●

TYING INSTRUCTIONS

Dave's 17-Year Itch Cicada

This pattern is the author's tried-and-true cicada pattern for periodical emergences. This pattern has been refined over Brood V, VIII, XIV, and X over the last two decades. It is a simple, durable, and realistic "enough" for all species of fish that eat cicadas. Tied in a range of sizes, this pattern will mimic all cicadas—annual or periodical—when tied in local cicada colorations.

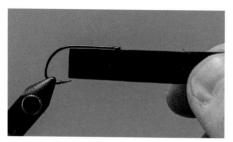

Step 1: Cut two pieces of black craft foam about 2 inches long and as wide as the hook gap. For a Gamakatsu B10S in size 4, as illustrated here, this results in a strip about ⅜ inch wide.

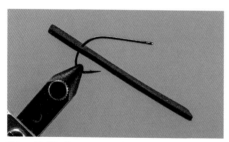

Step 2: Before mounting your hook in the vise, pierce the center of one of the foam strips about ½ inch from the end of the strip.

Step 3: Start the tying thread and build up a layer on the hook shank from just behind the eye to the start of the bend of the hook.

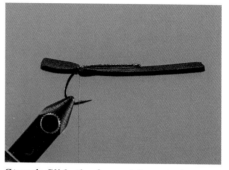

Step 4: Slide the foam strip onto the bottom side of the hook, with the short end facing the rear, to where the thread stops and make 2–5 wraps, securing the foam.

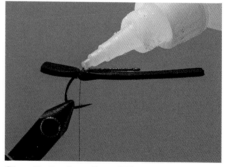

Step 5: Apply a dot of Zap-A-Gap to the tie-in point of the foam and the rear section of foam.

Step 6: Take the second strip and match the ends. Make 3–5 thread wraps over both strips to secure. It helps to compress the foam together to enable a wide, flat profile as the glue sets.

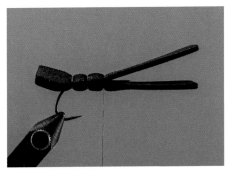

Step 9: Apply adhesive and secure the top strip with 3–5 wraps. Repeat steps 7–9 to create two equal segments. When viewed from the top or bottom, there will be uniform segments.

Step 7: Fold the long end of the top foam strip toward the back and advance the thread to the shank of the hook. Make 2–4 turns to create space where the next segment will begin. This distance will be approximately half the hook gap width.

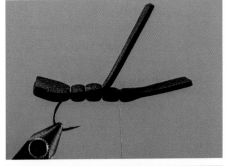

Step 10: Advance the thread to the shank and wrap to the hook eye. Secure the bottom strip to the shank with 3–5 wraps. Trim the remaining foam closely to the hook eye.

Step 8: Make 2–5 wraps securing the bottom strip.

Step 11: Wrap 5–8 more turns to secure the tag end created by trimming the foam. *Note:* I do not use glue on the final segment, as it sometimes blocks the eye of the hook.

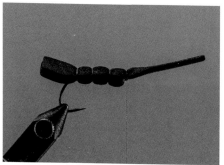

Step 12: Secure the top strip at the eye of the hook with 3–5 turns pulled tight.

Step 13: Advance the thread to the previous segment on the top side of the fly. Secure this wrap with 2–4 turns.

Step 14: Tie in 4–5 strands of pearl Krystal Flash on the far edge of the top foam with the ends just beyond the hook shank. Fold the forward-facing strands to create a second clump of fibers; this time, secure them on the close edge of the top foam. This creates two clumps on either side of center on the top of the fly. Trim both clumps to the same length.

Step 15: Cut a clump of natural elk body hair consisting of about 50 strands. Pull out any under fibers and stack to align the tips. Secure the hair with 3–5 tight wraps and additional wraps capturing the ends of the hair. This helps flare the hair more upright.

Step 16: Trim the ends of the elk hair and apply adhesive.

Step 17: Prepare a thin strip of red craft foam, as wide as it is thick, and about 1 inch long. Place this on the forward-facing top foam strip, fold the strip back, and pull tight. This creates the wing case and eyes. Secure with 5–7 wraps. Trim the "eyes" so they're slightly protruding from the width of the top foam sheet.

Step 18: Select two orange-barred Sili Legs and line the butts against the length of the wing and flash on the side of the fly nearest you. Tie in with 2–3 wraps. Fold the opposite ends around and tie in on the other side of the fly. Trim the legs to length as illustrated. I tend to leave the legs long and trim as needed. It is much easier to trim than add length!

Step 19: Secure in a ¼-inch-wide strip of orange craft foam for the indicator spot. Trim to length, slightly shorter in the front than in the rear.

Step 20: Trim the wing case to a "V" shape and trim the butt end to a point. Whip finish and apply cement to the final wraps.

Finished fly: When tying this and most cicada patterns, think of the profile from the fish's view. They need to be wider than they are tall, with legs that not only add to the imitation but also help stabilize the fly.

Dave's Dog Day Cicada

This fly is a great late-summer fly when the annual dog day cicada makes its appearance. It is completely made from synthetic materials and has an inner body to create a wider, fatter body profile. Tie this fly in an all-black variation in addition to brown and olive in sizes 6, 4, and 2.

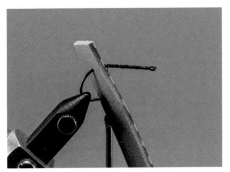

Step 1: Cut two pieces of craft foam about 2 inches long and as wide as the hook gap. For this variation, use olive foam for the bottom and brown for the top. For a Gamakatsu B10S in size 4, as illustrated here, this results in a strip about ⅜ inch wide. Before mounting your hook in the vise, pierce the center of the bottom foam strip about ½ inch from the end of the strip.

Step 2: Start the tying thread and build up a layer on the hook shank just behind the eye to the start of the bend of the hook. Apply Zap-A-Gap to the thread wraps and tie in the foam beetle body on the top of the hook shank. Secure with wraps along the entire shank. This is the underbody that will provide the wide profile.

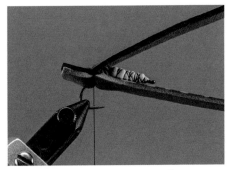

Step 3: Apply a dot of Zap-A-Gap to the tie-in point of the foam and the rear section of foam. Take the top strip and match the ends. Make 3–5 thread wraps over both strips to secure. It helps to compress the foam together to enable a wide, flat profile as the glue sets.

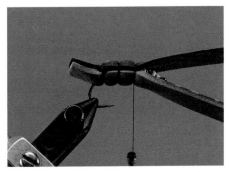

Step 4: Fold the long end of the top foam strip toward the back and advance the thread to the shank of the hook. Make 2–4 turns to create space where the next segment will begin. This distance will be approximately half the hook gap width. Make 2–5 wraps securing the bottom strip.

Step 5: Apply adhesive and secure the top strip with 3–5 wraps. Repeat this step to create three equal segments. When viewed from the top or bottom, there will be uniform segments

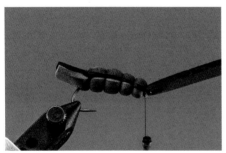

Step 6: Advance the thread to the shank and wrap to the hook eye. Secure the bottom strip to the shank with 3–5 wraps. Trim the remaining foam closely the hook eye. Wrap 5–8 more turns to secure the tag end created by trimming the foam. *Note:* I do not use glue on the final segment, as it sometimes blocks the eye of the hook.

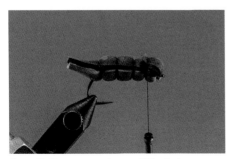

Step 7: Prepare a piece of black 1 mm thick foam about 1 inch long. Lay this across the front of the top foam strip above the hook eye. Fold the top strip back tightly and tie off. This will create the head and eyes. Secure with 5–7 wraps.

Step 8: Trim the "eyes" so they're slightly protruding from the width of the top foam sheet. Trim the foam at the tail end of the fly to a point.

Step 9: Tie in one strand of brown barred Sili Legs on each side of the body with 3–5 turns of thread. Advance the thread on the top of the body to the front of the second segment from the rear. Tie in the rear segment of legs to this segment with 3–5 turns. Advance the thread back to the third section, crossing over the top of the fly. Repeat for each side of the fly. You will see an "X" on the third segment when viewed from above. Trim the forward "leg" close to the body.

Step 10: Tie in 10 strands of pearl Krystal Flash and 5 strands of black Krystal Flash on the far edge of the top foam with the ends just beyond the hook shank. Fold the forward-facing strands to create a second clump of fibers; this time, secure them on the close edge of the top foam. This creates two clumps on either side of center on the top of the fly. Pull the ends of the material toward the back of the fly and cut off evenly at the point of the tail.

Step 11: Cut a clump of white Supreme Hair consisting of about 40 strands. Secure the hair with 3–5 tight wraps and fold the forward-facing strands to the rear, creating a second clump of fibers. Adjust the position so that two distinct "wings" are seen from above. Pull the fibers back toward the tail and trim evenly about ¼ inch past the Krystal Flash.

Step 12: Prepare a 1 mm thick piece of foam about ⅜ inch wide and 1 inch long. Cut a "V" notch in one of the narrow ends.

Step 13: Apply a small dot of adhesive on the wing fibers and tie in the foam with the "V" facing the rear of the fly. Secure with 3–5 wraps. Advance the thread to the next segment toward the eye of the hook and secure with 3–5 wraps.

Step 14: Tie in one set of brown barred Sili Legs with 2–3 wraps. Repeat on both sides of the fly. Trim to length, with the front set slightly shorter than the middle set.

Step 15: Advance the tying thread to the previous body segment, crossing over the top of the fly. Fold back the top piece of black foam and tie in, securing with 3–5 wraps.

Step 17: Using a leg knotting tool, knot the rear legs and trim to length. When tying this pattern, pay attention to the proportions of the segments, to avoid crowding the wings and legs at the front of the fly.

Step 16: Add a clump of white Para Post fibers for an indicator, and trim and whip finish.

Dave's Mountain Cicada

This pattern is a great general fly that can be used in a variety of situations. The original pattern I tied several years ago was an all-black variation with knotted legs to imitate a cricket. For the cicada variation, orange dubbing is substituted, as well as orange and barred leg materials. Using Senyo's Laser Dub with a spun dubbing loop allows for a brushy and "buggy"-looking body. Tied this way, it will provide an accurate imitation for the various "mountain cicadas" found across the Rockies, particularly Colorado's Front Range, Utah, New Mexico, Idaho, Montana, and Wyoming. *Okanagana bella* and *Platypedia putnami* are common species present in the West. The natural insect has a grayish cast and sometimes a hairy appearance. This pattern also works well in "hopper-dropper" rigs for general searching. I carry a few sizes of this fly whenever I am in the West during early summer.

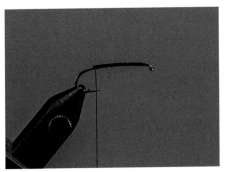

Step 1: Mount a TMC 2302 in sizes 8–12 in the vise and start your thread. Proceed to wrap a thread base along the entire shank, and advance your thread to just beyond the hook point.

Step 3: Wrap the dubbing rope two-thirds up the shank toward the eye and tie off. Trim excess.

Step 2: Form a dubbing loop, wax it, and apply rusty bronze Senyo's Laser Dub to the loop. Spin the loop to build a tight, tapered rope. Comb the loop gently and pick out any long, stray fibers.

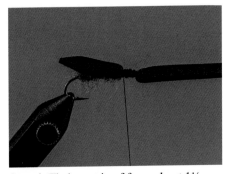

Step 4: Tie in a strip of foam about 1½ inches long and as wide as the hook gap. Cut a point at the end of the strip equal to the length of the hook. Tie in at the point where the dubbed body ended. Wrap thread toward the eye of the hook, compressing the foam along the shank. Advance thread back to the foam tie-in point.

Step 5: Select 5 strands of pearl Krystal Flash and 3 strands of black Krystal Flash, align the ends, and tie in to form a "wing" on the top side of the fly closest to you. Fold the remainder of the material to form a second wing on the top edge of the fly farthest from you. Lightly pull these fibers toward the back and trim to the length of the foam strip.

Step 6: Select a clump of light gray Para Post wing material and tie in to form two distinct wings as in Step 5. Trim slightly longer than the Krystal Flash material.

Step 7: Tie in an orange round rubber leg on the side facing you. Secure with 3–5 wraps and bring the forward-facing end of the leg around the top of the shank to the

other side, forming the opposite leg. Secure with 3–5 thread wraps. Trim the legs to the length of the Para Post wing material.

Step 8: Advance the thread to the front of the hook, just behind the eye. Wax thread about an inch and pinch-dub rusty bronze Senyo's Laser Dub.

Step 9: Wrap the dubbed thread one-third the distance toward the wing.

Step 10: Tie in a black-and-gray barred centipede leg right behind the dubbed section from Step 9 on each side of the shank.

Step 11: Wax thread about an inch and a half and pinch-dub rusty bronze Senyo's Laser Dub.

Step 12: Wrap the dubbed thread in between the legs and to the base of the wing. The dubbed sections in between the legs keep them evenly separated.

Step 13: Fold the tag end of the foam strip tightly over the top of the fly and secure with 3–5 thread wraps.

Step 14: Trim the foam to a "V" shape, forming the wing case.

Step 15: Prepare a small strip of orange 2 mm foam and secure with 3–5 wraps to the top of the fly. Whip finish and trim thread.

Step 16: Trim front legs to length. The front legs should be approximately three-fourths the length of the middle legs. This fly is much slimmer in profile, as it imitates many of the smaller varieties of mountain cicadas. Avoid tying this pattern too bulky. I sometimes leave the legs longer than shown, typical of attractor patterns. You can always trim them shorter on the stream.

RECIPES

Dave's 17-Year Itch Cicada

- **Originator:** Dave Zielinski
- **Tier:** Dave Zielinski
- **Hook:** #6-2 Gamakatsu B10S
- **Thread:** Fire orange 140-denier UTC
- **Underbody:** Black craft foam (2 mm)
- **Top, Head, and Back:** Black craft foam (2 mm)
- **Underwing:** Pearl Krystal Flash
- **Wing:** Natural elk hair
- **Legs:** Orange barred Sili Legs
- **Eyes:** Red craft foam (2 mm)
- **Indicator:** Orange craft foam (2 mm)
- **Adhesive:** Superglue or Zap-A-Gap

Notes: This is the author's time-tested pattern for any periodical cicada emergence. It has evolved over the years, mainly with hook availability and leg materials. Use glue in between foam pieces, tie-in points, and after wing materials are tied in. Tied in the smaller sizes (#6), it is a great, low-riding imitation of *Magicicada cassini* cicadas in the East, and in #8, of *Platypedia putnami* cicadas in the West.

Dave's Mallard Wing Cicada

- **Originator:** Dave Zielinski
- **Tier:** Dave Zielinski
- **Hook:** #6-4 Gamakatsu B10S
- **Thread:** Fire orange 140-denier UTC
- **Body:** Black craft foam (2 mm)
- **Top, Head, and Back:** Black Evasote foam (2 mm)
- **Underwing:** Gray Bett's Z-Lon
- **Flash:** Pearl Krystal Flash
- **Overwing:** 2 mallard flank feathers
- **Legs:** Orange barred Sili Legs
- **Eyes:** Strip of red craft foam (2 mm)
- **Adhesive:** Superglue or Zap-A-Gap

Notes: The Evasote foam in this pattern tends to give a higher-riding pattern. I prefer to use this on lakes when there is a little chop on the water. The mallard wings can be splayed out or folded back depending on what you are seeing on the water.

Dave's Septendecim Cicada

- **Originator:** Dave Zielinski
- **Tier:** Dave Zielinski
- **Hook:** #4-2 Gamakatsu B10S
- **Thread:** Fire orange 140-denier UTC
- **Underbody:** Dark brown craft foam (2 mm)
- **Top, Head, and Back:** Black craft foam (2 mm)
- **Segmentation:** Orange Antron dubbing
- **Underwing:** Yellow poly yarn
- **Flash:** Mix of black and pearl Krystal Flash
- **Wing:** Orange dyed elk hair
- **Legs:** Orange MFC Sexi-Floss
- **Eyes:** Red craft foam (2 mm)
- **Adhesive:** Superglue or Zap-A-Gap

Notes: I use this pattern in large sizes when the *Septendecim* are the dominant species. The underside of naturals is more orange brown than black, and this mimics the color and size well. The pattern also has high visibility to the angler. This was a secret weapon on the 2019 emergence of Brood VIII on my home waters in southwest Pennsylvania for carp and warmwater species. Have a few of these in your box to give the fish a break from the overall black-colored patterns. Sometimes a subtle difference in color incites enough confidence to force an eat.

Dave's Dead Cicada

- **Originator:** Dave Zielinski
- **Tier:** Dave Zielinski
- **Hook:** #10-4 Gamakatsu B10S
- **Thread:** Fire orange 140-denier UTC
- **Underbody:** Black craft foam (2 mm)
- **Top, Head, and Back:** Black Evasote foam (2 mm)
- **Underwing:** Pearl Krystal Flash
- **Underwing:** Gray Bett's Z-Lon
- **Wing:** Light dun MFC Mottled Web Wing
- **Legs:** Orange barred Sili Legs
- **Eyes:** Strip of red craft foam (2 mm)
- **Indicator:** Red or orange craft foam (2 mm)
- **Adhesive:** Superglue or Zap-A-Gap

Notes: This pattern works great late in the emergence. The wing material tends to soak up water, but the Evasote keeps it floating. This will ride low in the film, imitating the dying insect. Use "X" wraps and superglue to keep the wings splayed. Tie this pattern in smaller sizes (#8-6) for *M. cassini* periodicals in the East and *P. putnami* in the West.

Dave's Dog Day Cicada

Dave's Mountain Cicada

- **Originator:** Dave Zielinski
- **Tier:** Dave Zielinski
- **Hook:** #6-2 Gamakatsu B10S
- **Thread:** Black 140-denier UTC
- **Underbody:** Olive craft foam (2 mm)
- **Inner Body:** Foam Spider Body #4 (for #4 and 2 hooks) and #6 for #6 hooks
- **Top, Head, and Back:** Brown craft foam (2 mm)
- **Underwing:** Pearl and black Krystal Flash
- **Wing:** White Supreme Hair
- **Wing Case:** Black foam (1 mm)
- **Legs:** Brown barred Sili Legs
- **Eyes:** Strip of black craft foam (2 mm)
- **Indicator:** White Para Post
- **Adhesive:** Superglue or Zap-A-Gap

Notes: This pattern imitates the July and August "dog day" cicada. Other color combinations such as solid black and solid brown work very well. In addition, tie a white-bellied version and use markers to color match naturals.

- **Originator:** Dave Zielinski
- **Tier:** Dave Zielinski
- **Hook:** #8-12 TMC 2302
- **Thread:** Black 140-denier UTC
- **Underbody:** Rusty bronze Senyo's Laser Dub (substitute black to match local)
- **Overbody:** Black foam (1 mm)
- **Rear legs:** Orange round rubber (small)
- **Front legs:** Black/gray barred centipede legs (small)
- **Underwing:** 10 strands pearl and 5 strands black Krystal Flash, divided into 2 wings
- **Overwing:** Light gray Para Post
- **Indicator:** Orange foam (2 mm)

Notes: This easy-to-tie pattern is a staple in my western fly box. It originally started as a cricket pattern I have fished for many years in solid black. It is a fast, easy-to-tie pattern that puts fish in the net. The solid orange rear legs also mimic the prominent outer wing vein of the mountain cicada, *Okanagana bella Davis*, found in Colorado's Front Range, as well as *Platypedia putnami*, found in Utah, Colorado, Montana, Wyoming, and New Mexico. Tie this pattern in several sizes, from #8 for a great searching pattern to #10 and #12 for realistic hatch matching and pressured fish. Adult bugs have bodies that are approximately 20 mm in length, with wings stretching the bugs' total length to 30 mm.

Platypedia puntami: A common annual cicada of importance to fly anglers across the West.

| Rainy's Ultimate Cicada | Rainy's Ultimate Mormon Cricket |

- **Originator:** Rainy's Flies
- **Tier:** Rainy's Flies
- **Hook:** #6-2 TMC 8089
- **Thread:** Black 6/0
- **Body:** ⅜-inch sandable foam cylinder, shaped
- **Thorax:** Black hackle
- **Underwing:** Pearl Krystal Flash
- **Wing:** Bleached elk hair
- **Legs:** 1 pair orange barred black round rubber, 1 pair black round rubber
- **Eyes:** Doll eyes
- **Ovipositor:** Orange Loon UV cure fly paint

- **Originator:** Rainy's Flies
- **Tier:** Rainy's Flies
- **Hook:** #6-4 TMC 8089
- **Thread:** Black 140-denier UTC
- **Body:** ⅜-inch sandable foam cylinder, shaped, hollowed out with a rattle epoxied inside
- **Eyes:** Doll eyes (3 mm)
- **Collar:** Black hackle
- **Legs:** Black round rubber, knotted 3-strand rear legs, single front legs
- **Underwing:** Pearl Krystal Flash
- **Underwing:** Bleached elk hair
- **Overwing:** White Web Wing
- **Indicator:** Red craft foam (3 mm)

George Daniel Cicada (Greg Hoover variant)

- **Originator:** Greg Hoover, adapted by George Daniel
- **Tier:** George Daniel
- **Hook:** #6 TMC 5262
- **Thread:** Orange 6/0
- **Body:** Black craft foam (2 mm)
- **Underbody:** UV hot orange Ice Dub
- **Legs:** Black/orange Hairline centipede legs
- **Wing:** Flashabou: ⅓ pearl, ⅓ white, ⅓ orange (substitute Kreinik flash if desired)

Notes: This pattern is an updated version of Greg Hoover's original cicada pattern with modern materials. When building the wing, George combines the materials in his hands to achieve a more natural look versus a layered man-made look.

Cicada Chubby Chernobyl

- **Originator:** Allan Woolley, Mark Forslund; cicada adaptation by George Daniel
- **Tier:** George Daniel
- **Hook:** #4-8 TMC 5262
- **Thread:** Orange 6/0
- **Underbody:** UV hot orange Ice Dub
- **Overbody:** Black craft foam (2 mm)
- **Rear wing:** ½ orange and ½ white poly yarn
- **Legs:** Black/orange Hairline centipede legs
- **Front wing:** ½ orange and ½ white poly yarn, doubled

Notes: The original Chernobyl Ant was developed as a "one fly" tournament fly and has won that competition at least twice. It's a great searching pattern that will float in any kind of water, as well as a great fly for "hopper-dropper" rigs. It looks buggy enough and imitates several insects. In fast water, where fish do not have a lot of time to inspect flies and count legs, the Chubby excels. No box is complete without a few in various sizes.

Sinking Cicada

Jake's Brood X Cicada

- **Originator:** George Daniel
- **Tier:** George Daniel
- **Hook:** #6 TMC 5262
- **Thread:** Orange 6/0
- **Underbody:** 0.035-inch lead wire wrap
- **Rib:** 4X mono
- **Head and Overwing:** Black Furry Foam
- **Body:** Orange chenille
- **Legs:** Black/orange Hairline centipede legs
- **Wing:** Flashabou: ⅓ pearl, ⅓ white, ⅓ orange (substitute Kreinik flash if desired)

Notes: Similar to the Greg Hoover variation, when building the wing, George combines the materials in his hands to achieve a more natural look versus a layered man-made look.

- **Originator:** Jake Villwock
- **Tier:** Dave Zielinski
- **Hook:** #2 Partridge Sedge Caddis
- **Thread:** Amber 210-denier Danville
- **Underbody:** Black Thin Fly Foam (2 mm)
- **Body:** Black and gray Thin Fly Foam (2 mm)
- **Legs:** Barred amber MFC Sexi-Floss
- **Underwing:** Black and pearl Krystal Flash
- **Underwing:** White poly floating yarn
- **Wing:** Mottled brown Web Wing
- **Indicator:** Orange Thin Fly Foam (2 mm)
- **Eyes:** Red craft pins, trimmed with wire cutters and glued to the head
- **Adhesive:** Fly Tyers Z-ment

Notes: This pattern was developed by Jake Villwock of eastern Pennsylvania. Jake is a well-known guide in the area, specializing in fly fishing for smallmouth bass. Jake developed this pattern in preparation for the emergence of Brood X in June of 2021. This pattern uses readily available materials, and is a good balance of realistic features with function. Tie this pattern in all black with gray and green highlights for the annual "dog day" cicada found in late summer on Pennsylvania waters. Jake can be reached at his website, www.relentlessflyfishing.com.

Project Cicada

- **Originator:** Clark Pierce
- **Tier:** Dan Hill
- **Hook:** #4 Partridge Attitude Extra
- **Thread:** Orange 10/0 Veevus
- **Body:** Black cross-link foam (3 mm), cut with a large MFC Beavertail cutter
- **Wing:** Light dun Hairline Thin Wing
- **Overwing:** Fluorescent orange and dark gray Para Post
- **Indicator:** Orange Para Post
- **Wing Cover:** Black cross-link foam (1 mm)
- **Legs:** Speckled gray Hairline centipede legs
- **Eyes:** Melted #40 monofilament, colored with red Sharpie
- **Adhesive:** Zap-A-Gap

Card's Cicada

- **Originator:** Charlie Card
- **Tier:** Montana Fly Company
- **Hook:** #8 MFC 7000
- **Thread:** Black 6/0 MFC
- **Body:** Black craft foam (3 mm)
- **Underwing:** Rainbow Flashabou
- **Overwing:** White calf tail

- **Front Legs:** Orange barred Sili Legs
- **Back Legs:** Black MFC Sexi-Floss

Notes: This pattern is a simple, flush-floating cicada pattern that matches the smaller cicadas (*Platypedia putnami*) on Utah's Green River. Charlie Card is a longtime Green River guide who is well respected as an authority on the river, its surroundings, and cicada fishing.

Card's Green River Super Cicada

- **Originator:** Charlie Card
- **Tier:** Montana Fly Company
- **Hook:** #8 MFC 7000
- **Thread:** Black 6/0 MFC
- **Body and Head:** Black craft foam (2 mm)
- **Underbody:** Black/orange variegated chenille (medium)
- **Wing:** White MFC Widow's Web
- **Underwing:** Mylar sheet
- **Legs:** Orange barred Sili Legs
- **Hackle:** Grizzly dyed burnt orange
- **Indicator:** Orange foam (1 mm)

Notes: This is Charlie's souped-up pattern that floats high and is great for faster water and dropper-rig setups.

The Sickada Bomb—Periodical

The Sickada Bomb—Annual

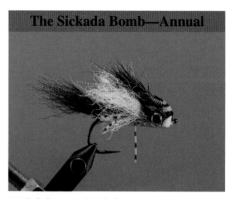

- **Originator:** Pat Cohen
- **Tier:** Pat Cohen
- **Hook:** #1/0 Ahrex TP610
- **Thread:** Black 210-denier flat waxed nylon
- **Body:** Orange and black layered, spun, and tightly packed deer hair
- **Tail:** Black bucktail
- **Tail Flash:** Copper Flashabou
- **Wing:** White calf tail
- **Wing Flash:** Copper Flashabou
- **Legs:** Orange barred centipede legs
- **Eyes:** Neon green with red pupil Designer Fly Eyes (³⁄₁₆ inch)
- **Adhesive:** Zap-A-Gap

Notes: Pat Cohen is a fly-tier extraordinaire, especially when it comes to tying with deer hair. He uses various tools for tying with deer hair that make tightly packed bodies possible. He offers these as well as materials on his website, www.rusuperfly. com. The flies pictured are Pat's own ties that he graciously provided for this book. This pattern can be adapted for endless color combinations. It works extremely well as a late-summer dog day bug, and can even be worked like a traditional bass popper. The head and wing shape allow it to make a wake when pulled, which is very effective when cicadas are on the menu and bass are looking up.

- **Originator:** Pat Cohen
- **Tier:** Pat Cohen
- **Hook:** #1/0 Ahrex TP610
- **Thread:** Black 210-denier flat waxed nylon
- **Body:** Neon green, black, dark green, and olive green layered, spun, and tightly packed deer
- **Tail:** Olive bucktail
- **Tail Flash:** Chartreuse Flashabou
- **Wing:** White calf tail
- **Wing Flash:** Chartreuse Flashabou
- **Legs:** Chartreuse barred centipede legs

Notes: See The Sickada Bomb—Periodical

Pinecone Cicada

- **Originator:** Clark Pierce
- **Tier:** Dave Zielinski
- **Hook:** #4 Firehole Sticks 618
- **Thread:** Black 140-denier Danville
- **Body:** Peacock black Ice Dub
- **Body:** Black Chicone's Fettuccine Foam
- **Head:** Black craft foam (2 mm)
- **Thorax:** UV shrimp pink Ice Dub
- **Wing:** Pale Morning Dun EP Trigger Point International Fibers
- **Underwing:** Pearl green Ripple Ice Fiber
- **Legs:** Orange Life Flex spandex
- **Indicator:** Orange craft foam (2 mm)
- **Adhesive:** Superglue

Notes: This innovative pattern comes from the vise of Clark Pierce of Riverton, Utah. Clark and Curtis Fry own Fly Fish Food in Orem, Utah, a super-stocked fly shop with internet sales and a series of blog articles and tying tutorial videos. The Pinecone Cicada pattern is probably the most unsinkable foam pattern available. The main body of the fly is made by spinning the Chicone's Fettuccine Foam similar to spinning deer hair. When forming the body, use a clump of eight strands, separated with the body dubbing material. Three separate sections will be sufficient to form the body. Apply superglue to the body and press it to make the clump of foam fibers stick together. Trim to a cicada shape after the glue sets. Tie this pattern in a variety of color combinations to imitate the periodical and annual varieties in your area. A tutorial of Clark tying this fly can be found at the website, www.flyfishfood.com.

Chuck Kraft Excalibur Classic Cicada

- **Originator:** Chuck Craft
- **Tier:** Eastern Trophies
- **Hook:** #2-4 Mustad CK52S
- **Thread:** Black 6/0
- **Body:** Chuck Craft cone-shaped cork, sanded flat on bottom and top, painted black
- **Weight:** 15–20 wraps of 0.030 lead wire
- **After Body:** Rusty orange Krystal Flash chenille
- **Legs:** Orange barred brown round rubber, orange rubber
- **Tail:** Black Game Changer tail (medium)
- **Eyes:** Red paint
- **Paint Markings:** Orange model paint, clear-coated with 5-minute epoxy
- **Topcoat:** Liquid Fusion

Notes: This pattern requires a significant time investment; however, it is unsinkable, extremely durable, and catches fish. Chuck Craft was a very well-known smallmouth guide and an innovative fly tier. He sadly passed away in March 2020. His legacy is being carried on by William Heresniak, owner and guide at Eastern Trophies. The materials for this pattern in addition to completed flies can be purchased from his website, www.easterntrophies.com.

Chuck Kraft Excalibur Dog Day Cicada

- **Originator:** Chuck Craft
- **Tier:** Eastern Trophies
- **Hook:** #2 Mustad CK52S
- **Thread:** Black 6/0
- **Body:** Chuck Craft cone-shaped cork, sanded flat on bottom and top, painted olive green
- **Weight:** 15–20 wraps of 0.030-inch lead wire
- **After Body:** Olive Krystal Flash chenille
- **Legs:** Olive round rubber
- **Tail:** Olive Game Changer tail (medium)
- **Eyes:** Black paint
- **Paint markings:** Purple, gold, and black model paint, clear-coated with 5-minute epoxy
- **Topcoat:** Liquid Fusion

Notes: See the Chuck Kraft Excalibur Classic Cicada

Chocklett's Cicada

- **Originator:** Blane Chocklett
- **Tier:** Blane Chocklett
- **Hook:** #4 Mustad CK52S
- **Thread:** 6/0 to match body color
- **Body:** Black Loco Skin, ³⁄₁₆-inch wide by 8 inches long
- **Underbody:** Spider body (size 4)
- **Head:** ¹⁄₁₆-inch craft foam
- **Wing:** Light gray Gummy Wing
- **Tymbals and Wing Case:** Black Loco Skin
- **Legs:** Olive round rubber (large), knotted
- **Eyes:** Ball-head pins: red for periodical, black or olive for annual
- **Adhesive:** Loctite superglue
- **Coloring and Markings:** Markers and nail polish
- **Overcoat:** Sally Hansen Hard-as-Nails, coat the entire fly except wings
- **Indicator:** ³⁄₃₂-inch orange indicator post glued on top of the head

Notes: This is a realistic pattern in size, color, and profile. The Loco Skin is tied in sticky-side up and wrapped over the spider body to give a segmented look and a wide, fat body profile. The use of modern materials, glue, and the kinked-shank popper hook all make for a great-looking and durable fly. Tie this in both periodical orange and black colors as well as black and olive annual cicada colors.

Chocklett's Cicada next to a male *Neotibicen linnei*.

Fused Body Cicada X

- **Originator:** Dron Lee
- **Tier:** Dan Hill
- **Hook:** #4 Gamakatsu B10S
- **Thread:** Black 6/0
- **Body:** Black closed-cell foam (3 mm)
- **Inner Body:** Any color foam (3 mm)
- **Adhesive:** Superglue or Zap-A-Gap
- **Markings:** Orange Loon paint
- **Wing:** Pearl Flashabou
- **Legs:** Orange barred black rubber
- **Eyes:** Red beads on mono

Notes: This very realistic pattern was developed by Dron Lee. He refers to this as a "fused body" fly, as two pieces make up the upper and lower body, joined by using a flame to "fuse" the edges. This piece is fit over the hook and inner body to provide a realistic shape and profile. This pattern can be tied in a myriad of colors representing dog day annuals using olive, black, or brown foam, or solid black to imitate periodical cicadas. Dron will use markers to accurately tint wing, body, and carapace portions of the bug. Because of its body profile, this pattern lands on the water in a very lifelike manner.

Granato's Chubby Muffin Cicada

- **Originator:** Nick Granato
- **Tier:** Rainy's Flies
- **Hook:** #6-8 TMC 5262
- **Thread:** Black 6/0
- **Underbody:** Rusty orange Senyo's Laser Dub
- **Body:** Black foam (6 mm)
- **Rib:** Red small UTC Ultra Wire
- **Overwing:** White calf tail
- **Underwing:** Black Krystal Flash
- **Legs:** Orange barred Sili Legs, brown sparkle Sili Legs
- **Eyes:** Red Mirage dome eyes (3/32 inch)

Whitlock's Periodical Cicada

Micah's Cicada

- **Originator:** Dave Whitlock
- **Tier:** Dave Whitlock
- **Hook:** #6 Daiichi 1260
- **Thread:** Red 6/0
- **Underbody:** Pearl Krystal Flash wrapped on hook shank
- **Overbody:** Black Spider body (size 4)
- **Rear Wing:** Pearl Krystal Flash
- **Front Wing:** 3–5 strands each of orange, black, and pearl Krystal Flash
- **Legs:** Amber barred Sili Legs
- **Eyes:** Red doll eyes (³⁄₁₆ inch)
- **Indicator:** ³⁄₃₂-inch orange cylinder glued to the top of head
- **Adhesive:** Superglue

Notes: Dave Whitlock needs no introduction and has fished this pattern over several periodical emergences in the East. This pattern has an accurate body profile and wings that are splayed. I carry a few of these late in the periodical emergence when fish have seen a lot of flies and may key on a specific profile. Having this pattern in my box matches when bugs are both upside down on the water and with wings open.

- **Originator:** Micah Dammeyer
- **Tier:** Micah Dammeyer
- **Hook:** #6 TMC 2312
- **Thread:** Orange 6/0
- **Body:** Orange and black craft foam, laminated with Zap-A-Gap
- **Head:** Black craft foam
- **Wing:** Orange Krystal Flash and white poly yarn
- **Legs:** Orange barred Sili Legs
- **Eyes:** Orange craft foam

Notes: Micah is a fly-fishing instructor, tier, and guide under the name Knee Deep Fly Fishing, located in the Washington, DC, area. He uses this fly for the periodic emergences the area experiences. This fly was a great producer for him during the emergence of Brood X in 2021. Laminate layers of orange and black foam in advance, then cut tapered body sections with a razor blade. The head is made from two pieces of black foam about ¼ inch wide. The first is pierced through the hook and pulled back across the side of the head, then the second piece is pulled top to bottom. Legs are threaded through the fly using a needle, just behind the tie-in point of the head. Use Zap-A-Gap on each step of the fly for durability.

Goodman's Pitboss Cicada

Clark's Cicada—Olive

- **Originator:** Clint Goodman
- **Tier:** Rainy's Flies
- **Hook:** #8 Ahrex FW560 or TMC 3761
- **Thread:** Black 6/0
- **Underbody:** Rusty bronze Senyo's Laser Dub
- **Overbody:** Black #4 foam beetle body
- **Wing:** White MFC Widow's Web
- **Front Legs:** Black round rubber
- **Rear Legs:** Orange round rubber
- **Indicator:** Fluorescent pink Bett's Z-Lon
- **Rib:** Red fine copper wire
- **Collar:** Orange Senyo's Laser Dub
- **Head:** Black foam (2 mm)
- **Eyes:** Orange mono

Notes: This pattern is a durable, high-floating, and effective imitation across the West. The profile imitates a cicada with its wings splayed on the water's surface. It's also a great pattern for fishing dropper rigs, as it is ultra-buoyant.

- **Originator:** Clark Reid
- **Tier:** Umpqua Feather Merchants
- **Hook:** #8 TMC 200R
- **Thread:** Olive 3/0
- **Body:** Olive deer hair
- **Wing:** Light dun Shimazaki fly wing
- **Underwing:** Pearl Krystal Flash
- **Legs:** Black round rubber (small)

Notes: This is a legendary pattern that comes from Clark Reid of New Zealand, which is known for summer-long annual cicada hatches of small olive and tan species. The original pattern did not have rubber legs. Tie this updated pattern in black for an accurate, durable, and low-floating imitation of mountain cicadas.

Grillos Hamburgler

- **Originator:** Andrew Grillos
- **Tier:** Dave Zielinski
- **Hook:** #8-12 TMC 3761
- **Thread:** Black 140-denier UTC
- **Body:** Peacock Ice Dub
- **Overbody:** Black foam (2 mm), doubled
- **Wing:** 50/50 mix of light gray and orange McFlylon
- **Legs:** Black round rubber, orange round rubber
- **Eyes:** Orange foam

Notes: The original pattern is a highly visible floating beetle pattern very popular in the West. The original uses all black legs and high-vis pink wings, which works equally well where smaller mountain cicadas inhabit western rivers. The double foam body keeps it floating high, while the heavier TMC 3761 hook stabilizes it so that it sits perfectly upright and low in the film. It's a great and simple western cicada pattern, and a great pattern for dropper rigs as well.

Grillo's Hippie Stomper Cicada Variation

- **Originator:** Andrew Grillos
- **Tier:** Dave Zielinski
- **Hook:** #8-12 TMC 3761
- **Thread:** Black 140-denier UTC
- **Tail:** Moose mane
- **Body:** 5 strands copper and 5 strands black Krystal Flash, wrapped
- **Overbody:** Black foam over orange foam (both 2 mm)
- **Wing:** Silver MFC Widow's Web
- **Legs:** Orange barred Sili Legs
- **Hackle:** Grizzly and rusty brown hackle

Notes: Andrew Grillo's Hippie Stomper has been a longtime, western favorite attractor pattern, especially in riffles or pocketwater. Andrew is a great innovator and known for tying flies that are simple, effective, and easy for both the fish and angler to see. This particular fly always seems to land upright and float like it should. When tied in black and orange, it has all the main ingredients for a cicada pattern—stout hook, low profile, high visible wing, and floats like a cork. I have used this pattern on many streams in Colorado's Front Range with great success.

A Colorado trout that fell for the Hippie Stomper in cicada clothes.

Umpqua Carl's Cicada

- **Originator:** Carl Stout
- **Tier:** Umpqua Feather Merchants
- **Hook:** #8-10 TMC 5262
- **Thread:** Black 6/0
- **Body:** Black craft foam (3 mm)
- **Overwing:** White calf tail
- **Underwing:** Black Flashabou
- **Legs:** Black and ginger MFC Sexi-Floss

Craven's Baby Boy Hopper— Cicada variation

- **Originator:** Charlie Craven
- **Tier:** Cody Eardley
- **Hook:** #12 TMC 2457
- **Thread:** Burnt orange 140-denier UTC
- **Body:** Black craft foam (2 mm)
- **Legs:** Orange/black Wapsi Barred Round Rubber (medium)
- **Wing:** Dark gray Para Post
- **Hot Spot Wing:** UV orange EP Trigger Point Fibers
- **Hot Spot/Wing Cap:** Orange craft foam (2 mm)

Pop Pop's Simple Cicada

- **Originator:** Robert Bell
- **Tier:** Robert Bell
- **Hook:** #4-8 Gamakatsu B10S or TMC 5262
- **Thread:** Orange 6/0
- **Body:** Black craft foam (2 mm)
- **Underwing:** Pearl Krystal Flash
- **Overwing:** Natural cow elk
- **Rib:** Orange fly line backing
- **Legs:** Orange barred black Sili Legs
- **Indicator:** Orange vernille

Notes: This pattern is a simplified, utilitarian fly that is tied sparsely. Bob will use whatever materials he has on hand to tie this, often substituting different colors or materials for the indicator, legs, or rib. Use your imagination and match this simple fly to the naturals in your area.

Hipster Doofus Cicada

- **Originator:** Paul Mason
- **Tier:** Rainy's Flies
- **Hook:** #6-8 TMC 3761
- **Thread:** Black 6/0 UNI-Thread
- **Underbody:** Black foam (2 mm)
- **Overbody:** Orange foam (1 mm)
- **Back:** Black foam (2 mm)
- **Rib:** 2 strands copper mylar
- **Head:** Peacock Ice Dub
- **Wing:** EP Fibers: equal mix of gold, black/ purple, and Holo silver
- **Legs:** Orange MFC Sexi-Floss, marked with black Sharpie
- **Indicator:** Orange foam (1 mm)
- **Post:** Light gray Para Post

Slim Cicady

- **Originator:** Dave Zielinski
- **Tier:** Dave Zielinski
- **Hook:** #8 Partridge Sedge/Caddis KT 12S
- **Thread:** Black 6/0 Danville
- **Body:** Black foam (2 mm), ⅜-inch-wide strip tapered to ¼ inch
- **Underbody:** Black 6/0 Danville
- **Wing:** Light dun EP Trigger Point Fibers

- **Eyes:** Gray foam strip (1 mm)
- **Indicator:** Orange foam (2 mm)
- **Legs:** Amber MFC Barred Sexi-Floss
- **Adhesive:** Loon UV cure, thin

Notes: This fly is a very light and flush-floating pattern. Trim the profile of the foam body to a rounded point to imitate the cicada profile. When the fly is complete, coat the underbody with the UV cure adhesive. This will secure the materials to the hook shank and keep them from rotating. This fly was a top producer on the Green River on a trip there in June 2021 when the *Platypedia putnami* cicadas were emerging.

Moodah Poodah

- **Originator:** Curtis Fry
- **Tier:** Curtis Fry
- **Hook:** #8-12 Daiichi 1160 Klinkhammer
- **Thread:** Black 6/0
- **Body:** Black and orange Ice Dub
- **Head:** Black Cross-Link foam (2 mm)
- **Tag:** Pearl Flashabou
- **Wing:** Black cow elk
- **Legs:** Orange barred centipede legs
- **Indicator:** Fluorescent orange Para Post
- **Adhesive:** Superglue

Notes: This fly was developed by Curtis Fry of Utah. Curtis and Clark Pierce own and operate Fly Fish Food in Orem, Utah. This pattern is tied a variety of color patterns to not only match cicadas, but beetles, crickets, and hoppers. This is a great pattern for fishing dropper flies off the hook bend.

Chubby Chernobyl Annual Cicada

- **Originator:** Allan Woolley, Mark Forslund
- **Tier:** Rio Products
- **Hook:** #6-8 TMC 5262
- **Thread:** Black 6/0
- **Body:** Peacock Ice Dub
- **Wing:** Light gray Para Post
- **Legs:** Black olive barred Sili Legs
- **Tail:** Black Krystal Flash

Ninja Cicada

- **Originator:** Rio Products
- **Tier:** Rio Products
- **Hook:** #8-12 Tiemco 200R
- **Thread:** Brown 140-denier UTC
- **Underbody:** Brown 140-denier UTC
- **Overbody:** Black craft foam (2 mm)
- **Underwing:** Pearl Krystal Flash
- **Overwing:** Bleached elk hair
- **Legs:** Brown round rubber
- **Hackle:** Grizzly

Hoover's Cicada

- **Originator:** Greg Hoover
- **Tier:** Dave Zielinski
- **Hook:** #8-6 Tiemco 5262
- **Thread:** Black 6/0
- **Body:** Orange chenille
- **Overwing:** Elk hair
- **Underwing:** Pearl Krystal Flash
- **Legs:** Orange rubber legs
- **Indicator:** Orange hi-vis Antron yarn (optional)

Notes: This pattern is likely one of the oldest known and widely used imitations for periodical cicadas. Greg Hoover, retired Penn State entomologist and fly-fishing author, developed this simple pattern many years ago during one of the central Pennsylvania emergences of Brood XIV.

Cork's Cicada

- **Originator:** Steve Ludwig
- **Tier:** Steve Ludwig
- **Hook:** #4-8 Gamakatsu B10S
- **Thread:** Black 140-denier UTC

- **Body:** Black foam (3 mm, top) glued to orange foam (1 mm, bottom)
- **Underwing:** Pearl Wing-n-Flash
- **Overwing:** Elk hair
- **Legs:** Orange barred Sili Legs
- **Markings:** Brown Sharpie marker on bottom
- **Adhesive:** Zap-A-Gap

Notes: Premake bodies by gluing a sheet of black 3 mm foam to orange 1 mm foam. Cut the body strips about ¼ inch wide for smaller sizes and ⅜ inch wide for the #4 hook. Use Sharpie markers to color the underside to match local cicadas.

Hubka's Foam Cicada

- **Originator:** Jerry Hubka
- **Tier:** Dave Zielinski
- **Hook:** #8-14 Tiemco 2312
- **Thread:** Black 140-denier UTC
- **Body:** Black craft foam (3 mm)
- **Wing:** White MFC Widow's Web
- **Legs:** Orange round rubber
- **Indicator:** Fluorescent pink foam (1 mm)
- **Adhesive:** Clear Cure Goo Hydro

Mike's Pennsylvania Cicada

- **Originator:** Mike Engelhardt
- **Tier:** Mike Engelhardt
- **Hook:** #4 Gamakatsu B10S
- **Thread:** Black 140-denier Veevus
- **Overbody:** Black foam (2 mm), ⅜-inch-wide strip
- **Underbody:** Orange/black Hareline variegated chenille (medium)
- **Flash:** 2 strands pearl Krystal Flash
- **Underwing:** White Congo Hair
- **Overwing:** White deer belly hair
- **Indicator:** Red foam (2 mm)
- **Legs:** Orange barred black Hareline Grizzly Flutter Legs
- **Adhesive:** Loon UV cure, thin

Notes: Mike Engelhardt is a longtime fly-fishing guide on the Youghiogheny River in southwest Pennsylvania. He and the guides at Laurel Highlands Guide Service are the most knowledgeable and skilled anglers on the river. Mike is one of the other "cicada crazed" guys I know. He and I have shared notes and fly patterns over the last several years. Mike's fly has accounted for hundreds of fish during Pennsylvania periodical cicada emergences. His pattern is low on flash, and the use of Congo Hair and the white deer wing makes for an easy-to-see pattern on the water. The variegated chenille is a nod to the original Greg Hoover pattern and allows the fly to sit low in the film. This is especially helpful when fishing for carp, as they sometimes have a hard time finding the hook on higher-riding patterns.

Fuzzy Cicada

- **Originator:** Dave Zielinski
- **Tier:** Dave Zielinski
- **Hook:** #12-8 TMC 5262
- **Thread:** Black 140-denier UTC
- **Body:** Black foam (1 mm)
- **Body Segments:** Rusty Antron dubbing
- **Wing:** Light dun Bett's Z-Lon
- **Indicator:** Orange foam (1 mm)
- **Flash:** 3 strands copper Krystal Flash on each side of wing
- **Legs:** Orange barred Sili Legs (fine)

Notes: The Fuzzy Cicada is a basic hopper pattern adaptation that can be used as a general searching pattern. The segmentation using dubbed thread provides a "buggy" look that imitates many of the smaller annual mountain cicadas that have a "hairy" appearance. Change the dubbing and leg colors from yellow to brown or black to imitate local cicada coloration.

Cicaddis

- **Originator:** Dave Zielinski
- **Tier:** Dave Zielinski
- **Hook:** #10-8 TMC 3761
- **Thread:** Black 140-denier UTC
- **Body:** Rusty orange Senyo's Laser Dub in a dubbing loop
- **Overbody:** Black foam (1 mm)
- **Wing:** Light gray Bett's Z-Lon with 2 strands orange Antron yarn on each side of main wing
- **Indicator:** Orange foam (2 mm)
- **Legs:** Orange barred Sili Legs

Notes: This pattern originally started out as a high-floating, high-visibility foam caddisfly that I would use on swift pocketwater streams for the native brook trout of the Laurel Highlands in Pennsylvania. For smaller annual cicada species, this fly is an excellent searching pattern. Tie a few in all black and even tan or olive variants to imitate not only cicadas, but other terrestrials like hoppers, beetles, and crickets.

EZ Wrap Cicada

- **Originator:** Dave Zielinski
- **Tier:** Dave Zielinski
- **Hook:** #8-6 TMC 2302
- **Thread:** Black 140-denier UTC
- **Body:** Brown, black, or olive foam (2 mm), cut in 3-inch-long strip tapered from ¼ inch wide to a point
- **Rib:** Amber UTC vinyl rib
- **Wing:** Natural cow elk hair
- **Underwing:** Copper Krystal Flash
- **Thorax:** Brown, black, or olive Senyo's Laser Dub
- **Eyes:** Black foam strip
- **Legs:** Black round rubber

Notes: This pattern is a quick tie, and is easier than it looks. Tie in the foam strip and vinyl rib at the bend of the hook, wind the foam forward to the thorax, and tie off. Wrap the ribbing material forward and tie off. Add flash, wing, and dub thorax. Fold tag end of the foam strip forward, tie off just behind the thorax, and add legs. If eyes are desired, add a small strip of foam before folding to make the head. This pattern hits the surface with a defined "splat" due to the football-shaped body profile. Tie this in all black or olive in larger sizes for a great late-season bug for matching dog day annuals.

Denny Breer Cicada

- **Originator:** Denny Breer
- **Tier:** Darren Bowcutt
- **Hook:** #8 Gamakatsu S10s
- **Thread:** Black 6/0
- **Overbody:** Black craft foam (2 mm)
- **Underbody:** Black Cactus Chenille (medium)
- **Underwing:** Black Krystal Flash
- **Wing:** Natural deer hair
- **Overwing:** White Antron yarn
- **Legs:** Orange barred Sili Legs

Notes: Dennis Breer, who tragically passed away in 2006, was a Green River icon. He was founder and owner of Trout Creek Flies and Green River Outfitters. Breer authored the book *Utah's Green River: A Flyfisher's Guide to the Flaming Gorge Tailwater* and was a longtime friend, mentor to guides, and advocate of the river and Dutch John. Few were more active in the conservation and management of the area than Dennis. He was also an innovator of terrestrial flies, many of them cicada patterns used on his home waters as well as across the West. This pattern came to me from Darren Bowcutt, a guide and personal friend of Dennis. Darren tells me this pattern has evolved over the years as materials have changed. Several variants exist, and two are included in this book. Dennis often advised leaving the cicada pattern on the surface for very long, undisturbed drifts. The natural often sits motionless on the water for long distances. He theorized that the fish will know the fly is fake if you keep moving it.

Denny Breer Cicada—Variant

- **Originator:** Denny Breer
- **Tier:** Darren Bowcutt
- **Hook:** #8 Gamakatsu S10s
- **Thread:** Black 6/0
- **Body:** Black craft foam (2 mm)
- **Underwing:** Black Krystal Flash
- **Wing:** Natural deer hair
- **Overwing:** White Antron yarn
- **Legs:** Orange barred Sili Legs, clear mottled Sili Legs

Notes: This variant is very similar to the original pattern but lacks an underbody for a slimmer profile. The addition of knotted legs and a clear set of legs imitate not only the legs of a natural, but the wing outline.

Daniel Seaman's Cicada

- **Originator:** Daniel Seaman
- **Tier:** Dan Hill
- **Hook:** #1/0 Daiichi 3111
- **Thread:** Orange 140-denier UTC
- **Body:** Black Cross-Link foam (6 mm), cut with River Road Creations Beavertail cutter

- **Head:** Black deer belly hair
- **Underwing:** Hot orange Para Post
- **Wing:** Natural mallard flank
- **Eyes:** Orange UV resin

Notes: This stout cicada pattern is tied on a super strong, heavy wire hook, resulting in a presentation that makes a loud "splat!" on the surface and rides low in the film.

Lovejoy's Clicker Cicada

- **Originator:** Brad Lovejoy
- **Tier:** Brad Lovejoy
- **Hook:** #10-12 Umpqua UC600BL-BN or Dohiku 301
- **Thread:** Black 6/0
- **Body and Head:** 3/16-inch foam, folded and glued over shank
- **Rib:** Brown copper wire (fine for smaller sizes, medium for others)
- **Underwing:** Dark elk hair
- **Wing Flash:** Black Ice fiber or black SLF
- **Overwing:** White, gray, light blue, and pink poly yarn brushed together
- **Legs:** Black rubber (fine), barred white
- **Collar:** Ginger furnace hackle, clipped on the bottom
- **Adhesive:** Zap-A-Gap

Notes: This Brad Lovejoy pattern is an accurate representation of the *Platypedia putnami* cicada found on the Green River in Utah where Brad is a guide. His fly is extremely well thought out, with durability and realism in mind. Note the muted colors—this species is black bodied with pale orange highlights. On a competitive fishery like the Green, the ginger hackle collar is just enough color to fool trout that have seen a lot of the brighter orange and black imitations. On the flies that Brad gave me, I noticed the elk hair wing is glued to the top of the body. Brad explained that it facilitates the profile of the fly on the water and adds additional durability. The use of the fine copper wire as a rib is a nice touch as it adds a little color and iridescence to the trout's eye view. The species that this imitates has a glossy black color on its belly, and the copper adds "just enough" shine and segmentation. Later in the season, when cicadas are aging, they tend to get lighter in color and their orange highlights fade. Consider tying this pattern using a dark gray foam and amber legs.

Lovejoy's Mondo Buzzer Cicada

- **Originator:** Brad Lovejoy
- **Tier:** Brad Lovejoy
- **Hook:** #2 Dohiku HDS
- **Thread:** Black 6/0
- **Overbody and Head:** Foam (4 mm)
- **Underbody:** Black and Orange Razor Foam strip, wrapped on hook shank
- **Rib:** Orange Bett's Z-Lon
- **Collar:** Ginger furnace hackle, clipped on bottom
- **Underwing:** Dyed black elk hair
- **Overwing:** White, gray, light blue, and pink poly yarn brushed together
- **Legs:** 1 pair black barred round rubber and 2 pairs orange MFC Sexi-Floss on each side
- **Adhesive:** Zap-A-Gap

Notes: This pattern is Brad's imitation for when the "mondo" cicadas are present on the Green. This species (*Okanagana magnifica*) overlaps and follows the smaller *Platypedia* species found on the river. The natural is supersize and a hearty meal for any trout. This is also a very durable pattern, using tough materials and adhesive at every step. Because of its size, consider using a barbless hook, as trout—even large ones—can get hurt significantly by large-size hooks. Barbless will slip out easily. *Pro tip:* Using a lighter, lightly heat the foam edges and compress them. This softens the hard, square edges and also seems to seal the pores of the foam, which helps the fly to not get waterlogged.

Jeremy Rogers Mondo Cicada

- **Originator:** Jeremy Rogers
- **Tier:** Jeremy Rogers
- **Hook:** #4 Gamakatsu S10
- **Thread:** Orange 140-denier UTC
- **Ovipositor:** Orange Fly Foam (2 mm)
- **Underbody:** Tan Fly Foam (2 mm)
- **Overbody and head:** Black Fly Foam (2 mm)
- **Underwing:** Pearl Krystal Flash
- **Wing veins:** Orange deer hair
- **Wing:** Black EP Fibers
- **Legs:** Amber MFC Sexi-Floss
- **Indicator:** Fluorescent pink Para Post
- **Adhesive:** Superglue

Notes: Jeremy Rogers owns and operates Provo River Guide Service. He spends his summers guiding on the Green at Flaming Gorge. This pattern is an accurate imitation of the "mondo" cicadas that occur yearly during June and July. The mondo, or "buzzers" as locals call them, are the *Okanagana magnifica* cicada. These are huge insects, with hairy black bodies, pale tan-orange highlights, and gray eyes. Not a quickly tied pattern, Jeremy's fly owes its durability to the use of superglue—a lot of superglue in every step of the process of building the fly. Feel lucky to hold one of Jeremy's personal flies in your hand; these don't get left behind in trees and snags.

Flutter Nugget

- **Originator:** Chris Krueger
- **Tier:** Montana Fly Company
- **Hook:** #8-10 MFC 7076
- **Thread:** Black 140-denier Danville
- **Body:** Black Fly Foam (2 mm)
- **Head:** Black deer hair, tied bullet style
- **Underwing:** Amber dyed mallard flank
- **Wing:** Black deer hair
- **Legs:** Orange barred centipede legs (small)
- **Indicator:** Orange foam (2 mm)

Notes: This pattern was developed by Chris Krueger in Colorado and matches common mountain cicadas on the Front Range, like *Okanagana bella* and *Platypedia* varieties. This pattern is durable and has an accurate profile to a natural cicada on the water with its wings folded. I like this pattern for its lack of flash materials, especially for pressured fish. This pattern is also very effective on other western waters like the Green River in Utah.

Okanagana magnifica: the "mondo" cicada of the Green River. COLBY CROSSLAND

Elvira Cicada

Panther Branch Bugs Annual Cicada

- **Originator:** Solitude Fly Company
- **Tier:** Solitude Fly Company
- **Hook:** #8 TMC 5262
- **Thread:** Black 6/0
- **Underbody:** Thread wraps
- **Body:** Black Fly Foam (2 mm)
- **Head:** Black Fly Foam (2 mm)
- **Underwing:** Rainbow Krystal Flash
- **Wing:** Light gray Antron yarn
- **Legs:** Black round rubber and orange barred, 1 pair on each side of the fly

Notes: This is a light and low-profile pattern that lands very softly on the surface when cast. I like this pattern for spooky or pressured fish that have seen a lot of flies.

- **Originator:** Brandon Bailes
- **Tier:** Brandon Bailes, Panther Branch Bugs
- **Hook:** #2 Ahrex NS122 light stinger hook
- **Thread:** Black 6/0
- **Underbody:** Peacock Ice Dub
- **Body:** Chocklett's Loco Foam
- **Wing:** Senyo's Predator Wrap and poly yarn
- **Legs:** Black round rubber (small)
- **Eyes:** Green craft pins
- **Indicator:** Yellow foam (1 mm)
- **Adhesive:** Flexible UV cure glue

Notes: Brandon is an expert fly tier and fly angler from northern Alabama. His innovative patterns have been developed on his home waters where he chases several species of native bass as well as smallmouth bass. His patterns are a great blend of durability, profile, and visibility. This fly has a fantastic profile on the water for a late-summer annual cicada pattern. It has accounted for some of his biggest bass over the last several years. This pattern has a place in my box as well; it closely matches the *Tibicen canicularis* and associated "dog day" species across much of the East.

Panther Branch Bugs Spent Cicada

Flip Flop Cicada Pop

- **Originator:** Brandon Bailes
- **Tier:** Brandon Bailes, Panther Branch Bugs
- **Hook:** #2 Ahrex NS110
- **Thread:** Black 6/0
- **Body and Head:** Natural, olive, and brown deer hair, spun, packed, and trimmed
- **Wing:** Barred clear Senyo's Predator Wrap
- **Legs:** Yellow round rubber (small)
- **Eyes:** Green craft pins
- **Tail:** Olive Gamechanger tail (small)
- **Adhesive:** Flexible UV cure resin

Notes: After trimming, coat the bottom and the collar of the fly with flexible UV cure glue to stiffen. This is a great looking, casting, and fishing fly. It is a softer-landing alternative to the Chuck Kraft Excalibur for when fish prefer a softer presentation. The wing composition in particular is a subtle but effective touch. The use of Senyo's Predator Wrap as a wing material is a key difference, as it is a softer, finer, and more flexible material, unlike many stiff wing fibers.

- **Originator:** Dave Zielinski
- **Tier:** Dave Zielinski
- **Hook:** #2 Gamakatsu B10S
- **Thread:** Black 6/0
- **Body and Head:** Black flip-flop foam, cut to shape, blockhead style
- **Tail:** Black EP Trigger Point Fibers and olive dyed grizzly hackle tips
- **Collar:** Olive dyed grizzly hackle
- **Legs:** Amber and gray MFC Barred Sexi-Floss, 4 each
- **Eyes:** Dome eyes (5/16 inch)
- **Adhesive:** Zap-A-Gap and Goop

Notes: This fly resembles a typical foam bass popper, but tied in black/olive to resemble the annual cicadas across the eastern and southern states. Use Zap-A-Gap to secure the foam to the hook shank and Goop to secure the eyes. Although this fly will "pop" with strips, fish it dead drift in all water types under trees and along banks when the sounds of annual cicadas are in the air.

Summer Screamer Cicada

- **Originator:** Dave Zielinski
- **Tier:** Dave Zielinski
- **Hook:** #4-2 Dohiku HDS
- **Thread:** Black 6/0
- **Body and Head:** Black and white craft foam (2 mm)
- **Tail:** Black craft foam strip (2 mm by 2 mm)
- **Underwing:** Black EP Fibers and 3 strands pearl Krystal Flash
- **Overwing:** Moose mane
- **Rear legs:** Lime-green centipede legs, knotted
- **Front legs:** Black round rubber, knotted
- **Eyes:** Yellow craft pins, darkened with a brown Sharpie
- **Belly Markings:** Black Sharpie
- **Adhesive:** Zap-A-Gap

Notes: This fly imitates any of the many green and black annual cicada varieties found across the South, East, and Midwest. Most of these bugs are shades of black and brown, often with frosty white bellies. Change coloration with foam colors or markers to match local species.

B52 Cicada

- **Originator:** Dave Zielinski
- **Tier:** Dave Zielinski
- **Hook:** #2 Gamakatsu S10
- **Body:** Orange (2 mm) and black (4 mm) foam cemented together, cut and sanded to a teardrop cicada shape
- **Wings:** Pearl and copper Krystal Flash
- **Legs:** 2 pairs black round rubber, 1 pair orange round rubber
- **Eyes:** Yellow push pins, colored red with a Sharpie marker
- **Adhesive:** 5-minute 2-part epoxy to secure hook to foam body, Zap-A-Gap to secure legs and wing material, contact cement to laminate body material

Notes: This fly is the only pattern included in this book that doesn't employ the use of thread. It is entirely constructed using glues. Prepare the body material by laminating several strips of orange and black foam using contact or rubber cement. Once cured, trim the body shape to match hook size, then use a small sanding block with 150 grit sandpaper

Summer Screamer Cicada next to the real thing, *Neotibicen linnei*.

to smooth and round the edges. Heat the foam with a lighter and brush with your fingertip to further smooth the edges. Cut a slit in the bottom of the body and use 2-part epoxy to secure to the hook shank. Coat the entire bottom side of the fly with the epoxy to add durability, and use the remainder of the glue batch to secure the eyes in place. Once dry, use a needle to thread the wing and leg materials through the body in the appropriate places. Use a dot of Zap-A-Gap at each leg and wing where it enters the body to secure. This fly is a bold pattern that lands with less of a subtle "plop" and more of a "crash landing" of a B-52 bomber. It's a fun summertime bass bug when tied in various colors.

Sneaky Pete Annual Cicada

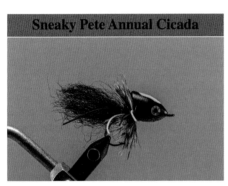

- **Originator:** Dave Zielinski
- **Tier:** Dave Zielinski
- **Hook:** #4-2 Mustad 3336
- **Thread:** Black 6/0
- **Body and Head:** Wapsi Perfect Popper head (#1-2 for #2 hooks, #4 for #4 hooks)
- **Tail:** Black EP Fibers
- **Rear Legs:** Green and black round rubber, 1 pair on each side
- **Front Legs:** Green and black round rubber, 1 pair on each side
- **Collar:** Olive dyed grizzly hackle
- **Eyes:** Pearl stick-on eyes
- **Indicator Spot:** Cyan acrylic brush-on paint or nail polish
- **Adhesive:** Epoxy
- **Paint:** Krylon spray paint: white or almond for the belly, gloss black for the top and head

Notes: No bass box is complete without a selection of Sneaky Petes. I am not sure of its true origins; however, Gaines Poppers, located in Gaines, Pennsylvania, has been making them since the 1950s. What makes this fly special is the way it can be worked. It is a hard-body "slider"-type fly that when pulled with quick strips will swim beneath the surface and float back to the top. Worked with a very slow twitch, the fly will make a subtle wake, with its rubber legs undulating, begging for a strike. Tied in the colors in the recipe and photo, this is an excellent smallmouth bass fly for late August when the dog day cicadas are abundant.

To build this pattern, use premade cupped and tapered popper bodies, but epoxy them to the hook backward. Once the epoxy sets, use painter's tape to mask the exposed hook and spray-paint the underside white or almond. When the belly color is dry, spray the top and sides gloss black, being careful to not cover up the belly color. Perhaps the best-kept secret is the use of the cyan indicator dot. This color is extremely easy to see on the water; it resembles nothing in nature that occurs with any regularity, and can be seen in low light. The human eye sees wavelengths between about 375 and 750 nanometers. Right in the middle of the color spectrum is about 500 nm, which corresponds to "traffic light green," which is a mix of blue and green, very close to cyan. Traffic lights are not their color by accident! The low profile of this fly and the fact that the top side is black make it nearly invisible, especially on long casts from the boat to the bank. Try the cyan and you will be amazed. Allow the color coats to dry and finish with a clear acrylic top coat. This will ensure the colors will stand up to many casts and fish. When annual cicadas are abundant, cast long, fish beneath mature trees, and work it with minimal movement.

Cork Annual Cicada

- **Originator:** Dave Zielinski, inspired by Chuck Kraft's Excalibur
- **Tier:** Dave Zielinski
- **Hook:** #2 Mustad CK52S Popper Hook
- **Thread:** Black 140-denier Danville
- **Body:** Cork, hand-shaped to a teardrop shape
- **Tail:** Black EP Fibers
- **Collar:** Black Spirit River Frosted Yarn
- **Legs:** Neon green round rubber (medium)
- **Adhesive:** Devcon 2 Ton Epoxy to adhere the hook to the cork, E6000 to secure legs to body
- **Markings and Paint:** Acrylic craft paint: black over a white base coat; olive, fluorescent green, yellow ochre, brown, and black to simulate cicada patterns. Krylon acrylic spray paint: clear gloss to clear-coat body.

Notes: I made this fly as a nod to the great Chuck Kraft during the August annual cicada season on my local waters. Start with a block of cork from a stopper or wine bottle. Using an X-Acto Razor Saw, cut into a smaller block, then sand and shape with 80, 150, and 220 grit sandpaper. Using the razor saw, cut a slit just deep enough to fit the hook shank. Secure the hook to the body with 2 Ton Epoxy and set aside for 24 hours. For a smooth finish, fill the cork with a wood putty and let dry. Once dry, sand with 400 grit paper and inspect the body under strong light to identify any pits or holes. Refill and sand as needed. Using an artist's brush, coat the entire cork body in a white acrylic paint. Once dry, coat the top and sides with black paint. Add designs using the brown, olive, yellow ochre, and other colors to simulate a cicada's markings. It does not need to be accurate. I prefer to use the brightest color on the top of the head where the bug will be facing you, so that you can see it. Once all colors have been added and dried, tape off the eye and bend of the hook with painter's masking tape. In a well-ventilated area, spray several coats of clear gloss Krylon spray paint to lock in the colors and make the fly much more durable. Be sure all of your paints are acrylic, as mixing oils or lacquers with acrylic will cause runs or adhesion issues. Once the fly is dry, tie in the tails and insert the legs using a sewing needle. Position legs as needed and use a bodkin to apply a small amount of E6000 glue to secure them as well as seal off the entry point.

Fishing Cicada Patterns

AFTER I SAID IT, A WASH OF GUILT RUSHED THROUGH MY BODY. I FELT SO dirty that no number of showers with a pressure washer would cleanse me of my guilt.

The three of us pulled our one-man pontoon boats out of the river, where we encountered four anglers looking hot, tired, and defeated, derigging their rods on the tailgate of their trucks. "How many did you get?" Bob asked the anglers. "Oh, we did okay, maybe four or five apiece," one of the men responded. Puzzled with his answer, I asked, "Really? On cicadas?" The anglers said they really didn't see any fish taking them, so they fished subsurface caddis nymphs. While it is true you won't find trout holding position like they typically do during a dry-fly hatch, make no mistake, the trout were indeed eating cicadas. They just weren't in their typical trouty places. They were hugging the banks, lying in the shadows under the sycamore trees and low limbs waiting for a cicada to drop. Another angler in the group asked, "How did you guys do?" He was in disbelief

The author, not high-stick nymphing, but holding the rod high to get a drag-free drift to entice an eat from a trophy trout on a cicada. COLBY CROSSLAND

125

and maybe a little disgusted when I said, "I don't know, I lost track. Maybe 60 or 70?" My moment of guilt hit instantly when I saw the expression on his face. I should have downplayed my excitement a bit. This is how it can be with cicadas and trout.

RIVERS AND STREAMS

I was blazing down the highway on a Friday after work, windows down, "London Calling" by the Clash blaring on the radio of my beat-up old Ford pickup. I was headed toward central Pennsylvania to meet my group of fishing friends for a full week of camping and fishing, hoping to encounter . . . you guessed it . . . cicadas, when my phone rang. "How far are you?" I heard on the other end of the line from a more-excited-than-normal Bob Bell, calling to give me the on-stream report and tell me where to meet him. He had finished a short day of work and was already on-stream, scouting and fishing. I've made this drive a thousand times and could give you an exact ETA from any point on the road. "I'm about an hour out," I responded. It sounded like we had a bad connection, as he was yelling gibberish through the phone. "Is that noise what I think it is?" I asked. I could make out "*cicadas*" when he hollered back. I pulled the truck over, closed the windows, and shut off the stereo to hear better, as this conversation was serious business worth listening to. The rest of the conversation went something like this:

Dave: "Are fish eating 'em?"

Bob: "Yup."

Dave: "How long have you been there?"

Bob: "About an hour or so."

Dave: "How many did you catch?"

Bob: "Oh, I don't know, a dozen or fifteen."

Dave: "Okay, I'm about 40 minutes out."

A Spring Creek rainbow on a Pop Pop's Simple Cicada fly, 2008 Brood XIV. Note the heavy tippet. Big flies, reckless fish, and hard eats warrant telephone cable tippet.

Bob claims he could hear my foot hit the gas pedal to the floor as I threw it in drive and hung up the phone. Somehow my ETA went from a 1-hour drive to a 40-minute drive. Cicada mania is real!

This was during the 2008 emergence of the 17-year Brood XIV periodical cicada in central Pennsylvania. This area is known for the best trout fishing in the state of Pennsylvania, with Penn State University at the center of it all. Famous streams such as Spring Creek, Penns Creek, the Little Juniata River, and Spruce Creek are all located in this area within an hour of one another. These are all cold, spring-fed limestone streams, easy to wade; most have excellent access and all are full of fish. We spent a total of 20 days fishing this emergence and sampling the action on all the creeks in the area.

The approach to fishing these and similar small to medium-size streams is primarily wading. Remember the sights and sounds when picking a location to fish. Listen for the unmistakable chorus of a cicada congregation, and look for bugs on the streamside vegetation and trees. On rainy or cooler days, or in the early morning, you will hear very little, but by inspecting the undersides of leaves and tree limbs, you will find the insects. On hot, sunny days, there is no need to get on the water early. Cicadas are most active during the hottest parts of the day, and it is never too hot for cicadas. This is when you will see flying bugs and hear the congregation singing. Because the cicada is a terrestrial insect, it may not occur on the entire river system. I like to check various spots, starting either high upstream or downstream and working my way back until I find the bugs. Take a walk, look for signs of emergence (holes at the base of old, mature trees, exoskeletons clinging to tree trunks), and check the undersides of leaves. Pay attention to sunlight and temperature. Read chapter 2 on scouting and research!

Once you locate the bugs in numbers by either sight or sound, match your fly's size to a natural and start scanning the water for any activity. It is normal to not see the entire stream boiling with fish activity. Look for subtle rises in the shadows of overhanging brush, trees, and structure. Look for fish "on the hunt" swimming through pools just under the surface. Lastly, pluck a natural from a tree limb and send it down the river and watch! It's okay; we've all done it!

You can fish upstream or downstream when fishing cicada patterns. My preference changes depending on the river and structure. On small to medium-size streams, a typical upstream presentation works well. Wading upstream is less likely to spook holding fish. For trout fishing I find it is a 50/50 game of blind casting and sight fishing with cicadas, like any terrestrial. You may see fish eating the bugs and hunting for them; these are easily targeted fish, typically not requiring a precise presentation. Laying the fly down with a little force so it hits the surface just like a natural will trigger a strike from fish keyed on the insect. I have seen trout move 20 feet to eat a cicada! If blind casting, fish all the water. The bugs cannot control where they fall in the water, and they will be everywhere. If you happen to be lucky enough to find a streamside tree where prolific numbers of bugs are congregating for mating, you will often find pods of fish hanging out in that area. It is not uncommon to catch several fish from one pool in this scenario. Of course, on more pressured waters, or with "experienced fish," the approach may need to be more delicate. If you are getting refusals or inspection rises, change or downsize your pattern, lighten your tippet, rest the spot, and try again. An interested fish is likely an eater unless it is totally chased off.

In medium-size to large streams and rivers, I prefer to wade downstream or float. It is less strenuous to walk downstream with the current instead of against it. On rivers where

Fishing from a drift boat allows access to fish unreachable on bigger waters as well as locating less pressured fish.

I can get to the middle and work my way down, I have the opportunity to throw flies under mature trees on both banks in addition to fishing the water below me. If fishing downstream, remember to delay your hookset, as the fish's open mouth is facing you.

Float fishing from a drift boat, raft, or other watercraft is an enjoyable way to cover a lot of water, spend the day with your fishing partners, and gain access to harder-to-reach sections of rivers and streams. Harder to reach often means less pressured fish as well. When floating a river, however, you will likely encounter sections absent of cicadas. Recall that they are commonly localized in mating groups, which may be far away from the water in certain areas. Use your ears to listen for the chorus. One side of the river may have bugs for 100 yards and the other side nothing. On the next river bend, you may find the opposite bank has bugs for a mile. During the late summer, singular trees may have a lot of singing as mating commences. Remember, you are only hearing the males; there are likely twice as many if not more cicadas present during peak mating activity. We will often yo-yo across the river as we hear the choruses to be near where the bugs are. A fish that is keyed on cicadas will be looking for the bug and will remain in the general area where they find most of them. Cicadas are where you find them! Even on sections where I am not hearing or seeing bugs, I will still fish the cicada and, typically, still catch fish.

There are a few reasons for this. First, and this is obvious, bugs are always being washed downstream. If you just came through a section with billions of screaming cicadas, it is very likely that well below that section there are still some bugs present in the water. Second, I have fished consecutive days where I have returned to a location that had great fishing and bugs one day and fewer the next day, with more in another location upstream or downstream. This is very often on the front end of an emergence and toward the end of mating. Continually scouting for new areas throughout the emergence cycle is a good plan. Colby Crossland, a guide at Spinnerfall Guide Service on Utah's famous

Green River, also will fish the cicada fly on water where the bugs are seemingly absent. He believes the fish have a memory, as they see fishable numbers of annual cicadas every year. The trout seem to be "imprinted" with the hunger for a cicada and will eat it when it presents itself.

When casting from a drift boat, raft, or other watercraft on a river with moderate current, practice the ability to cast long with a minimum of false casts. The rower is working hard to hold the boat just slower than the current in a line matching the caster's distance. False casting is wasted effort for both the angler and the rower, not to mention the missed opportunities in between fly placement. In addition to efficient casting, "line hand" management is equally important. When shooting line, keep the line hand close to the reel hand at the end of the cast. This ensures your line hand is ready to strip-set or twitch the fly, especially in moderate to fast current. I have witnessed hundreds of misses due to line-hand mismanagement—fish that blow up on the fly the instant it hit the water, but the caster wasn't ready—fly line all over the deck, the caster looking down at the line and missing the eat. The most efficient casters leave little line on the deck after the cast and are aware of the line in their hand, never having to look away from the fly. Always waiting nervously for the eat.

As summer closes in and the annual cicadas make their appearance, the summertime flows on rivers and streams are often lower than during springtime and early season hatches. Fish get a bit more wary, and boat noise and wakes can put off otherwise willing fish. This time of year, casts need to become longer. I tend to position my boat at the comfortable limit of the caster's abilities to the likely holding water. It can be a challenge to accurately drop a sizable cicada pattern on the surface with the right amount of disturbance, especially when casting far. In oxygen-rich, boulder-filled, fast water, I'm less concerned with a subtle presentation; often an authoritative *SMACK*! will draw attention

The infamous Steve Ludwig with a brown trout that took a cicada during Brood V

to the surface in broken water. In slower water, I am of the belief that fish are inherently aware of what is on the surface within a surprisingly wide range, having seen wakes from 10 feet away charging a well-placed fly. I would rather err on the side of subtle in this water type. I like to position my caster to target likely cover—boulders, points, rocks, and grassy banks where expert ambush predators like to wait for a bug to fall from the sky. This is especially true when floating rivers in late summer for smallmouth bass, but it works equally well on trout water, too.

When casting from a drift boat, fish the water ahead of the boat; again, the rower and caster are a team working to get a long, drag-free drift. Casting perpendicular or behind the boat often creates a belly in the line, dragging the fly downstream. Eats in this scenario are total luck or total loss. Fish will either hook themselves under the weight of the line or be a total miss, with the angler desperately trying to recover line and set the hook. Fish ahead of the boat and continually mend line to keep minimal slack between the rod tip and fly. I also believe that fish are aware of the boat's position further in advance than you may think. I have watched the waves of disturbance from rowing or a rocking boat travel across the surface and alert fish to the fact that something is up. I rarely fish alongside the boat unless the casts are long, and prefer a steeper angle downstream to the bank during cicada season. Remember, these fish are looking for something on top and may be more aware of surface disturbances than at other times of the year.

Cruising Fish

In rivers and streams, fish tend to face into the current, as it is a primary feeding direction, bringing food directly to their face. In lakes, fish have to resort to hunting and their senses of sight and vibration to locate prey. Often, lake fish are covering large amounts of the water's surface; you may see a rise in one location and see the same fish more than cast away eat the next fly. Be observant before casting. Try to locate a fish from a high vantage point or use a spotter who can see higher than you to direct your cast when fishing on high banks or land. In a boat, standing on an elevated deck is a game changer.

Once the fish is located, try to see the direction of travel and plant the fly ahead of the fish a few feet. When fish are hunting for cicadas, they tend to want to move a bit farther than with smaller mayflies and other insects. I have seen poor fly placement, leading a fish by 10 feet or more, still result in hookups. However, this is not always the case. Trout, specifically, usually cruise right under the surface, reducing their effective cone of vision. I have placed flies within a foot of a trout just as it turns the opposite direction, with the fish none the wiser the fly landed there. If you find an actively feeding fish, watch it, wait for it to feed, anticipate its direction of travel, and plant your fly 3 to 4 feet ahead of it. The same tactic works on bigger river systems with large eddies and trout circling, not holding in any particular position.

Another tactic, especially for trout, is to fish multiple flies. Fishing two dry flies increases the odds that a fish will find your fly and provides an opportunity to fish two different patterns and sizes. When I fish multi-dry-fly setups, typically for trout, I will use a slightly shorter leader, a foot or so less than the rod length, with the larger fly tied to the leader. Add a 3- to 4-foot piece of 2X or 3X to the bend of the hook and tie on the second fly. Be prepared to slow the cast down to avoid tangles. On windy days—all too common on lakes—increase the tippet sizes. Not only can you typically can get away with it without the fish seeing your leader, but it's easier for the tangling—or *untangling*—that frequently results with casting multi-fly setups.

Lake Fishing

Contributed by Robert Bell

As we rowed my drift boat across the small lake, I tried to prepare my 16-year-old son Chase for what we were going to encounter today. We were fishing during the Brood VIII emergence in a lake I had fished just a couple of days earlier. The fishing that day had been outstanding, as I caught carp—big carp up to 25 pounds—until my arm ached! Now I know what you are thinking, I have read those stories too and doubted them, but let me assure you, this one is true! As a matter of fact, on that day while landing the last fish of the day, I had to turn the 8-weight over and fight the fish with my left arm and reel with my right-hand upside down and backward!

Chase and I were headed to a location on the edge of a high cutbank with mature trees and a gradually sloping bottom that ends in a deep drop-off. Similar to a saltwater flat, with a mature forest on the shallow end and a deep channel on the other end. The water depth was less than 1 foot at the shoreline to about 4 feet 20 yards out from shore where it then dropped to 30 or more feet very quickly. This is one of my favorite location types for finding fish cruising looking for food on the surface. Everything comes together here. You have the food source, cicadas mating and singing in the trees, right next to the water with enough depth that the fish feel comfortable cruising the shallows knowing that the deep water is close by.

We anchored a long but comfortable cast from shore, approximately 60 feet, right over the drop-off and waited. In this situation we were hoping to find carp that were cruising the shoreline looking for cicadas that have mistakenly got in the water. In the shallow of a flat you can see the carp sometimes a hundred yards away, working their way down the shoreline, often

Chase and Bob Bell with Chase's first carp during Brood VIII in 2019

Chase Bell with another monster during Brood VIII, 2019. BOB BELL

disappearing into the depths and reappearing a few yards later. In the sun, the golden-brown backs of the carp stand out against the bottom. Additionally, you can often see them push water as they "drive" around inches under the surface looking for a helpless bug. As they approach, as single fish or in small groups of two or three, you typically have time to prepare for the cast when they are in range. As I pointed the first group out to Chase, I could see him tense up when he realized that these were not small fish. It took the trio of carp about two minutes to cover the 80 yards or so between us, as they would slowly cruise the shoreline then swim in or out to eat a cicada. They can appear almost schizophrenic, as they don't want to miss a potential meal. These were happy fish—no fear, just riding the buffet down the bank. It can sometimes be challenging to figure which direction they are going to be heading when they are in casting range, almost like a school of bonefish on a flat.

As the three carp were closing the gap between us, I coached Chase to anticipate the direction they would be facing and to pick a spot about 6 to 8 feet in front of them to drop his fly. I instructed him to lay the fly with a "plop" to attract their attention like a real cicada crashing into the water. By the time they were in casting range, I could see Chase was quite excited, and with a good case of "buck fever" he dumped his first cast on top of the school! They quickly departed for deep water, but not to worry, there would be plenty more shots.

It wasn't too long after and we had a pair of good fish cruising into casting range. This time Chase made a great 30-foot cast, laying the fly 5 feet in front of the lead fish. Instantly, both fish exploded to beat each other to the bug! Now this is where cicada fishing for carp gets interesting! Carp normally feed on the bottom in the mud, not on the surface for a dry fly. They are plain horrible at surface feeding! They tip straight upright to maybe a little over on their backs in the water and use their pectoral fins to move forward toward the fly. The whole time their sucker mouth and whiskers are trying to suck or sweep the bug into their mouth. This whole process can take from 5 to 30 seconds and sometimes feels like an eternity. Some fish will even leave the fly, swim away, then return for a second shot! It is great fun to watch this until it is your fly the fish is trying to eat! This can fry an angler's nerves, especially when the fish is one of the biggest of their life. I had already coached Chase to wait until the mouth had closed on his fly and the carp was turning down just a little before raising his rod, and he did this wonderfully. The fish went into his backing headed for safety in the depths of the main lake. Five minutes later we slid the 20-pound behemoth into the net. We went on to repeat this for the remainder of the day, including several double hookups. It was a day father and son would not soon forget!

Lake fishing can seem intimidating at first, especially with fly rods and dry flies. When fishing lakes during the cicada emergence, it becomes a shoreline game where the land is more important than the structure in the water. The first goal is to find areas where bugs are congregating. My favorite way to achieve this is to motor along the shoreline beyond casting distance and stop every quarter to half mile to listen. The best time to do this is five to eight days after first emergence to ensure bugs will be flying and male cicadas singing. The best days are warm and bright—70 degrees or higher. The males' chorus starts shortly after daylight and goes until the bugs are in the shadows of sunset. By motoring around the lake and stopping frequently, you will hear where the greatest concentrations of bugs are. When you locate bugs close to the water, approach slowly and quietly. This is where you will start to look for fish working the bugs that end up in the water. Sometimes the bug concentrations will be hundreds of yards from the water. These mating clusters of cicadas will likely not have enough bugs that make their way to the water to create fishing opportunities. Search until the chorus of bugs gets loud; you will have to raise your voice to have a conversation when cicadas are close by. When you cut the motor to listen for screaming bugs in the distance, cup your hands behind your ears and find the direction of major concentrations. It can be tough on the water, as the sound of cicadas is seemingly coming from everywhere, but with patience and frequent scouting, you will find the direction to motor toward.

In 2020 we were scouting a new lake during a Brood IX emergence when we cut the motor to drift and listen at the entrance of a long, narrow cove. Mark said, "This cove is full of singing cicadas, I am sure of it!" We quickly fired up the motor and ran another 400 yards up the skinny cove, then cut the motor. Before the hum of the outboard had stopped, the cicada chorus was already ringing in our ears; there were bugs all around us! We could see them flying from one side of the 100-yard-wide cove to the other. We observed bugs trying to cross the gap appearing to get exhausted. They would slowly lose height until they crashed into the water near shore. Just where a bug had crash-landed, an orange pair of lips poked up and searched frantically for the large protein meal. "Did you see that?" asked Mark excitedly, but I didn't have to answer, as he could see I was already ripping line off my 8-weight reel and getting ready to make a cast.

We believe protected coves are excellent places to search for fish that are actively feeding on cicadas. Typically, these areas are protected from wind, and on the lakes that we fish, narrow coves mean steep banks. Steep banks typically mean deep water is nearby. The reduced wind

Bob Bell with a lake-caught rainbow trout. This fish was out hunting the surface for the big bugs. BOB BELL

Bob Bell with a nice mirror carp during Brood IX in 2020. BOB BELL

also allows the angler to see on the water as well as hear better. Once a few cicadas start singing in a cove, the sound reverberates from everywhere seemingly at once, calling all other cicadas to the mating party. The bugs fly back and forth from treetop to treetop, and some occasionally drop in the water. Eventually, most of the fish in that area of the lake will be aware of the daily buffet of bugs on the surface. Go slowly around these coves even though there are cicadas everywhere. There will be certain places where they are closer to the water or the wind blows them in, and the fish will be working these areas searching for the large meal. Sneak up on these areas and you may be able to pick several fish off the edges. Run through them with your boat, and the fish may not be back for an hour or more. Coves with concentrations of fish can be great locations to anchor up and wait for passersby. If the fish are more scattered, trolling around the perimeter may be more effective.

As good as coves are for large mating congregations of cicadas, points of land projecting out into a lake can be better. "Did you see that blow up?" Blake asked excitedly! At the end of a long point into the main lake, where the land narrowed to just a skinny piece of gravel, several small-mouth bass had pinned a school of bait against the shoreline and were throwing water as they crashed into the bait. I cranked the trolling motor to the highest setting as Blake began peeling line from the reel on his fiberglass 8-weight tipped with a cicada. Less than a minute later, when we got within casting range, you could still see the smallies pushing water as Blake prepared to drop a fly near them. His fly landed about 2 feet to the side of the smallies' wakes, and as soon as it landed there was a push of water toward his fly. The first one there got not only the "meal" but also an exclusive invitation to be in a grip-and-grin photo with Blake. These bass were not hunting cicadas that morning, but upon finding one nearby, they did not hesitate to pounce at the opportunity.

Early in the cicada emergence, these points of land seem to be particularly attractive to mating cicadas and the fish that target them, provided they have mature tree growth present. They are among the first areas along shorelines that get good numbers of singing and mating cicadas.

Our observation is that the point of land receives more sunlight than surrounding shorelines, and thus the ground warms more quickly. In scouting missions at the beginning of emergence, we have seen these areas full of bugs while more shaded regions of the landscape have just started to show signs of emergence. The mating chorus coming from a long point can be heard by all of the freshly emerged cicadas on other, opposite shorelines. They attempt a long flight, and some end up crashing into the water near the shoreline along the point. As the numbers build, more and more bugs find their unfortunate way into the water. We usually find the first feeding fish of an emergence around long and narrow points with mature trees present.

Coves and points are not the only places to look for fish targeting cicadas on lakes. Sometimes a mile-long shoreline with a large tree or shrub that is bent over the water a little closer than the others can attract a mating cluster of cicadas. When looking for tree types, look for deciduous trees or even short shrubs. One such shrub about 30 feet or so tall had hundreds to thousands of cicadas in and flying around it. Any bug that fell, slipped, or made a mistake ended up in the water. Each day we fished Brood X we found 40 to 60 carp in a feeding frenzy under this tree. Several days in a row we could pick off 3 or 4 fish before the rest wised up to the game, then we would motor off in search of the next concentration of bugs and fish.

Another great place to look for fish targeting cicadas is flooded timber. On one trip I whispered to my 18-year-old son Clay, "Look back in those woods under that bush. There is a big fish feeding in circles under it." After several attempted casts, the big fish pushed into more open water, and Clay laid an imitation about 4 feet in front of it. A strange pair of lips came up and engulfed his fly, and the fight was on. During this emergence of Brood VIII, we had had several summer rainstorms, and the flooded lake had backed up into the trees and bushes where the cicadas were mating. Don't overlook flooded timber or anywhere the water meets trees to find fish targeting cicadas. The lake had a bit of color on this day, and we didn't see the fish Clay was fighting for ten minutes or so. We were concerned he had foul-hooked the fish because he just couldn't control him. Eventually the fish tired and we got our first look at how huge it was. Our

Blake Docter with the opportunistic smallie that was chasing bait in the shallows but didn't hesitate to eat the cicada pattern. BOB BELL

woefully small net would only hold its head past the pectoral fins. By tailing it and lifting its front half with the net, we were able to get the 46-inch grass carp into the boat. Such are the tales of fishing during a cicada emergence.

We spend a lot of our time looking at topo maps and Google Earth images, scouting shorelines for the right type of land *and* lake structure. As mentioned, steep banks usually mean deep water, especially in flooded man-made impoundments. Using these tools to locate the right topology can lead to success and large numbers of fish. Another great place to spend time looking for fish targeting cicadas is along deep drop-offs. Fish love the cover of the deep water and don't mind cruising the first 6 to 10 feet off the bank looking for cicadas that have fallen in. They swim just inches under the surface and seem to appear from nowhere, then dissolve back into the deep water when they are spooked by an errant cast or just sense danger. If the steep bank above the water has mature trees, it is a good place to slowly row or cruise along with the trolling motor looking for signs of eating or hunting fish. Often these fish will hug the bank within inches. Identify the direction the fish is swimming and plant your fly 2 to 4 feet ahead of it, right on the edge. Typically, these fish are casually hunting and eating slowly along their way; they don't often seem to be in any hurry. This makes for fun fishing, especially for young or new anglers.

I spent a day once with 14-year-old Kody and his mom, both new fly anglers. It was at the tail end of the peak activity during the Brood X emergence. The numbers of singing cicadas were noticeably less, but fish were still looking for them. With fewer bugs on the water, we decided to target the steep banks to locate cruising fish. We cut the motor as we got close to an area where I knew from the past couple of weeks there would be carp targeting cicadas. Kody's fly-fishing career had been limited to small bass and bluegills on his fly rod at local farm ponds. I knew

Clay Bell with the behemoth grass carp that was feeding in flooded timber during Brood VIII, 2019 (likely an escapee from a local golf course pond during high water). BOB BELL

Dave Zielinski and Steve Ludwig doubling up during Brood X, 2021. There was a third fish, but someone had to take a photo! BOB BELL

large carp would be challenging for him, but with shaking knees and after several blown casts, he finally got the idea to lead the fish, let it eat the fly, and then set the hook. The smile on that kid's face was priceless when we netted his first carp—an 8-pounder!

Despite the aforementioned target areas, the obvious advice is to look for fish feeding on cicadas anywhere they happen to be. Cicadas that end up in the water can be pushed by waves and end up on shorelines devoid of singing bugs. One time, by luck we found an area like this on a frustratingly windy day. A high vantage point from a boat, standing on a cooler with a high sun, can assist in finding working fish. Pay attention to fish working in these areas, and look for bugs caught in the surface film, as these places can be dynamite fishing!

On another occasion, the three of us rounded a corner into a cove and found six to eight boats tied up together like the "redneck yacht club" from country singer Craig Morgan's hit song. This was a serious party—swimming, drinking, and blasting music. We were set to fire up the motor and leave to find quieter waters when one of us noticed a school of large carp cruising near the surface, just two double hauls from the party barge. We dropped the trolling motor, and within a couple of minutes the three of us were tied to big carp with rods bent fully to the cork. When we slid the last of three carp into the same net, the yacht club gave us a big cheer and raised a cup to our success! We held all three fish up for a triple grip and grin for the party squad.

This was not a spot we normally would have targeted, but the cicadas were on the water and the fish were there. There were hundreds of cicadas washed along the shoreline from waves and at least 80 to 100 carp working this particular bank. We got 10 to 12 carp before the rest of the fish got wise to our game and left the area. We came back to this spot several times over the next couple of days, but never found bugs in the same concentration or any fish working the beach again. The point is the bugs were there and the fish were feeding on them. Keep your eyes open and pay attention to your surroundings. Some days you are better off being lucky than good, and we were glad we didn't miss fishing with the redneck yacht club! ●

GEAR

Rods

All cicada patterns are large, typically wind-resistant foam or deer hair bodies with legs and wings. Periodical cicada and late-summer annual "dog day" cicada patterns are huge bugs requiring a heavier line and leader to effectively cast them. In addition, the largest, hardest-fighting fish in the water will be eating them. Match your rod to the size of flies you will be fishing and in anticipation of the fish that will be eating them. I opt for rods no lighter than a 5-weight for trout and a 7- or 8-weight for bass and carp. If I had to choose one rod, it would be a 9-foot 7-weight. Casting big foam dry flies on a 7-weight is a joy and will handle most freshwater fish and all sizes of cicada patterns.

Modern graphite fly rods have taken advantage of materials science, enabling them to be lighter, stronger, and stiffer—or "faster to recover." These rods are excellent for throwing big, wind-resistant imitations, especially in windy conditions. Modern graphite is not the only material that excels for fishing cicada patterns, though; fiberglass fly rod technology has come a long way since its inception as well. Modern fiberglass is much faster and lighter than its former generations, with the added benefit of lifting power. New materials and processing methods have enabled lighter, longer, and stiffer fibers, creating glass rods that are superior to their predecessors. Nothing lifts heavy fish from the depths like fiberglass. Offshore tuna and pelagic rods are often fiberglass or a fiberglass/graphite mix because of its toughness and ability to lift. I believe it is a superior tool, especially for fighting big fish like 20-plus-pound carp in lakes where they will make multiple runs, dive deep, and drive their heads into weeds and muddy bottoms. The parabolic action of glass allows it to "bend into the cork," which facilitates lifting. Graphite rods of modern design typically have more of a tip action and stiffer butt sections that aren't as forgiving. I have experienced fewer break-offs, fewer bent hooks, and faster fish landing using modern fiberglass fly rods.

In 2020, while fishing the Brood IX emergence of periodical cicadas in southern Virginia, Bob Bell, his son Clay, and I fished to common and grass carp that pushed the scales to 30 pounds. The rod everyone wanted to fish when they were on the casting deck was the fiberglass 8-weight. We could literally cut our fish landing time in half using glass, with few worries of break-offs or straightened hooks. I believe on this trip, I coined the "30-second whip job" on a double hookup with Clay Bell.

We had simultaneously picked off two identical twins from a pod of cruising carp. Clay was fishing a fast-action graphite 8-weight, and I was fishing the fiberglass rod. I said "time me" to his dad, and it was 30 seconds to the net. Fish would eat the fly, blow up on the hookset, run to the deep water behind us, and show a bit of backing once or twice before giving up to the net. Clay fought his fish another minute and a half before landing. In a conversation with Mike Engelhardt, fly-fishing guide with Laurel Highlands Guide Service, I learned that his experiences were the same: "Nothing fights big fish like glass." Everyone wants that glass rod on the boat when we are fishing for carp. Glass and graphite rods are a mainstay in my arsenal, and I select the right tool for the job. When we are fishing for big fish, it is almost always with glass!

In trout situations, the typical medium- to fast-action 9-foot 5- or 6-weight fly rod will generally suffice. Often the annual cicada patterns in the West, like the mountain cicada or Putnam's cicada that occur in Colorado, Utah, Arizona, and New Mexico, are smaller. The smaller patterns, ranging from a size 8 to 12, can be presented well with

The arsenal for cicada fishing includes modern graphite and fiberglass fly rods.

The author just about ready to land a carp whipped on fiberglass. Not only are modern glass rods fun to fish, but you get extra style points for translucent blanks! BOB BELL

Clay Bell with his fiberglass stick in full send mode

lighter rods. Generally speaking, the setup you would fish during hopper time will suffice when presented with cicada opportunities. I sometimes will use a fast-action 7-weight on windier days and when fishing from a boat or raft.

Lines

Lines are simple for cicada fishing. A standard, good-quality, weight forward floating line is perfect for all situations and fish species. Use a line rated for your rod that you are comfortable casting. On modern graphite rods, you can slow down some of the some of the speed and soften the stiffness by lining up one size. If you have a super-fast-action 8-weight saltwater rod intended for windy flats fishing, try a weight forward 9-weight floating line and the rod will slow down. This can help with presentation, wind, and on-the-water line control, especially with large dry flies.

Leaders

Leaders can be extremely simple for fishing cicada flies. I prefer a leader as long as the rod in most situations, as there rarely is a need to go longer during cicada season. A store-bought tapered leader to 0X to 3X will suffice for most situations. I rarely fish purchased leaders, instead choosing to tie my own. I prefer a knotted connection to attach to the fly line and blood knots to join all leader sections. I like a knotted leader that can easily be repaired or adjusted as needed. If you find yourself getting refusals or needing to go lighter, clip the tippet section back to 18 inches or so and add 3 feet of the next-size-lighter tippet. This will generally get you in the ballpark for an easy casting and decent presentation of the fly.

The formulas for cicada leaders are shown below, based on fly size and line weight. The formula for 2X/3X leader is a slight variation of the George Harvey leader formula that has stood the test of time. I tuned it slightly to handle the larger, wind-resistant cicada patterns. You will note that I prefer Maxima Chameleon for the butt section of my leaders and any soft mono or fluorocarbon for tippet sections. Maxima is a stiff, hard mono leader material that has a brown color. It can be straightened by pulling it hand to hand over your knee, resulting in a stiff, straight leader that can transfer energy to turn a large foam or deer hair fly over. I have never attributed a refusal due to the brown color of the material; I don't think fish see it as intrusive. It is a color that fish are used to and is low glare when light hits it, taming reflections. Longtime steelhead anglers have used Maxima for ages on fish that have a tendency to be extremely line and tippet shy. In terms of mono or fluorocarbon, it is dealer's choice—use what you prefer. Fluorocarbon diameters per pound strength vary between brands and grades of material. I prefer the Yo-ZURI brand of H.D. fluorocarbon, as it has the smallest diameter per pound strength.

The leader formula below for the heavier fly line sizes is a simple three-section leader. I use this leader not only for fishing larger cicada patterns, but for most of my topwater smallmouth bass fishing and beach snook fishing on 7- and 8-weight fly rods when throwing Clouser Minnow–type flies.

LINE WEIGHT	FLY SIZE	LEADER SIZE	FORMULA
5-6-7	12-8	9 feet 2X or 3X	36 inches .020-inch Maxima Chameleon
			24 inches .017-inch Maxima Chameleon
			16 inches 0.13-inch Maxima Chameleon
			8 inches .010-inch Maxima Chameleon
			24 inches .008-inch (3X) standard clear mono or fluorocarbon
			or
			24 inches 0.009-inch (2X) standard mono or fluorocarbon
7-8-9	4-2	12-16 pound	48 inches .022-inch
			24 inches .017-inch
			36 inches #12-16 (0.011–.015-inch mono or fluorocarbon)

ADDITIONAL TACTICS

For the unfortunate cicada that falls in the water, it is the end of the line. In very few circumstances have I seen them able to recover themselves from the surface under their own power. In rivers and streams, flowing water will sometimes push them through seams to edges, and the lucky cicada may be able to catch streamside vegetation or debris. While they are in the water, they sometimes sit silently with their wings folded, and others will extend their wings and flutter, trying to escape the surface tension of the water. A cicada lying on its back on the surface faces a certain death. Typically, you will see these lying with wings splayed out as they await being eaten or washed away. They are very poor at locomotion on the water, but will cause quite the commotion when they flutter, which is certainly "ringing the dinner bell" to the predators below. In some cases, especially in

An excellent selection of "dog day" cicada patterns, and a couple of real ones for reference, too.

lakes, you will witness explosive rises to these bugs, as the fish seemingly believe the bug is getting away. Scan the surface, and look for these rises and bugs making a commotion. They are often dead giveaways to fish targeting the bugs.

Despite this reaction, it doesn't necessarily mean you should twitch your patterns constantly. In sight fishing situations, especially on lakes with carp, you will generally see groups of fish hunting. As you will recall, carp are at a disadvantage visually when looking at the surface. If you see the fish passing your fly, it may be that they did not see it. A single twitch or slight raising of your rod tip will drag the fly a few inches and almost always turn their heads. Carp know what they are looking for and have highly evolved sensory anatomy that allows them to find it. Sight, sound, and vibration will all trigger a response. However, resist the urge to fish your fly like a chugging bass bug popper. The natural bug does not pop or spit water with movement, and fish keyed on the hundreds or thousands of cicadas on the water will dismiss your pattern as a fake.

This is especially true during late-season bass fishing with prolific annual dog day cicadas around. These bugs are very large and can be imitated with a size 4 or 2 foam cicada pattern, Boogle Bug, or Chuck Kraft's Excalibur cork-bodied flies in black, bronze, or olive. Color and exact size do matter little; however, presentation is important. Dead drifting the pattern along likely holding spots—rock edges, brush, and cover—will result in surprisingly delicate eats quickly exploding into airborne bass of eye-popping size.

Not all twitching is bad, however. Late in the game, when the availability of cicadas begins to wane, it will take more and more effort to find fish eating them. At this point, fishing becomes similar to other types of terrestrial fishing, such as hoppers or beetles. Try twitching the fly intermittently with long pauses in between. The commotion on the surface may trigger a fish to look up, identify the fly, and eat it. This may also be a great time to start fishing cicada-dropper rigs, with your favorite or seasonally correct nymph imitation tied 12- to 18 inches off the bend of the hook. Very likely, you will take fish on both flies, similar again to late-season hopper fishing.

In a conversation with George Daniel, author and fly-fishing instructor, he shared insight to fishing for pressured fish. On George's home waters in central Pennsylvania, the local trout see a lot of flies—many of these spring creeks are open year-round, and on any day of the year you can find fish and anglers. It takes no time for the trout to understand that some food bites back. In conditions like this, George often fishes a subsurface cicada just a few inches beneath the surface, to convince a trout that it is safer to eat than the thousands of fly patterns floating overhead. George compares this to the effectiveness of sunken ants, which are extremely effective. George's pattern of choice is a basic Greg Hoover pattern with the shank wrapped in 0.030-inch lead wire. George also stacks the wing materials in his hand to elicit a natural effect versus a "man-made" layered look. His patterns are shared in the fly-tying chapter of this book. No box is complete without a few sinking or "waterlogged" patterns for highly pressured fish.

Epilogue

Ode to Cicada
I hear it sing
Its summer song
But never for all summer long
And when
That summer song is through
Just two wings left
One for me
And one for you

IT IS AUGUST 2022 AS I WRITE THE FINAL WORDS FOR THIS BOOK. THE DAY-light hours are beginning to wane, the younger kids are lamenting the approach of school starting, and the older kids are looking forward to going off to college to begin their next chapter in life or returning to meet the friends they missed during summertime back home. I'm looking into settling in to the coming fall, cutting grass for the last time, cleaning out gardens, and getting ready for fall bird hunting seasons with the return of woodcocks on their southern migrations. Soon I'll be getting back into the "two-handed swing of things" with the arrival of Great Lakes steelhead in the tributaries that fill Lake Erie.

In the last few years, we survived the COVID-19 pandemic and witnessed massive changes in world events and significant changes in ecosystems. Huge forest fires way ahead of fire season occurred across much of the West, historic drought and dewatering of hydro-dam lakes caused power brownouts in California, and a never-before-seen flash flood event changed the landscape of Yellowstone National Park. Nonetheless, more people are spending time outdoors than ever before. Fly fishing exploded during the pandemic, as well as an entire population reconnecting with the outdoors across America, bringing newcomers outside. This brings benefits and challenges to the outdoor world: The more that people experience and love it, hopefully the more they will value and protect it. On the flip side, it means increased pressure, which already has changed the woods and water through human presence. Our national parks have seen record attendance levels, which in turn means more dollars for local economies, a boom in guide services, and dollars for the park service to build and maintain trail systems, roads, and infrastructure. It also brings record crowding, full parking lots, timed-entry permits, and, in terms of fishing, a bit more difficulty in finding seclusion. For the willing and able, it means "go earlier, go longer, go farther." Chasing cicadas is an oddball aspect of fly fishing and, thus far, enables that attitude.

It has been a year without periodical cicadas in Pennsylvania where I reside, and having been spoiled by their presence the last three years in a row, I did miss their calls in early summer and the fishing that ensues. We are now in the "dog days of summer," and the first of many annual cicadas have begun their mating calls. My friends and I have been patiently waiting, watching closely, exchanging texts, listening, and wandering around trees looking for the signs, hoping to capture a glimpse of one of the many

The author in his early 30s fishing Brood XIV in 2008. Periodical cicadas will age you 13 or 17 years each time! BOB BELL

The release, and the end

species of beautifully colored green and black bugs. The fish are waiting too. The days are getting shorter, and the angle of light is triggering them to start feeding to prepare for the impending seasonal changes.

I did a little scouting recently on my local bass and warmwater river on my paddle-board, intently listening for sounds and paying close attention to sights along the river. I found several bass—some of them of good size—waiting in the shallows, idly looking for something. My hope is that they were waiting for the big-ticket meal item to drop out of the sky and find its way into their pool. "This week, it ought to start" I said to my friend Nate, as I have pumped him up and primered him with stories of smallmouth bass eating the annual cicadas in what can only be described as "toilet flushing" eats. I've been spending early mornings before work and late nights sitting at the vise, tying old familiar patterns and inventing new ones with the flashy new materials, fibers, hooks, eyeballs, and arseholes that hit the market this year, hoping to create the "lock picker" pattern that fish can't refuse. Just like the cicadas have evolved over millions of years, our fly patterns continue to evolve, whether through new materials, observation on the water, or a collaboration of ideas gathered up while sitting around the campfire telling stories and lies about cicada time.

I look forward to the coming years that bring periodicals back in the East, and we've already started to make plans around the bugs, places, and people that will make it all happen. Although 2023 is without periodicals, you can be assured that trips are being planned to the West for annuals on some of those rivers—named here and not—to meet up with the trout that eat them. I look forward to a reunion with friends on the Green, setting my watch to the cadence of annual cicadas on that amazing and beautiful river and targeting some new locations along the way in Colorado, Wyoming, and Montana.

The year 2024 will bring periodicals back to the Midwest with a once-in-221-years clash of 13-year and 17-year periodical cicadas. Broods XIII and XIX will overlap somewhere in the Midwest and will surely attract media attention, creep out kids, light up biologists, make cicada-eating social media superstars go viral, and certainly bring fish up. It is already time to start researching locations, digging up data on waterways, and building a hit list on where and when to target them. I don't think I have ever looked so far in advance to schedule time off from a day job for anything else in my life.

Then, 2025 will be an exciting year with Brood XIV returning to central Pennsylvania on what I refer to as my "home away from home waters." This will take little effort to coordinate but will surely provide a secondary data point to the last time I fished this emergence. I can imagine the intensity of our obsession will be pretty high in early spring as we fish the normal mayfly and caddis hatches, and recount stories of last time as the impending emergence starts around the end of May. I recently looked at the photographs from 2008 and recalled how fantastic the fishing was, with a secondary reaction of "damn, we were just puppies back then." I am hoping for a wet spring with rivers full of cold water enabling trout-friendly fishing until the Fourth of July. I do, however, anticipate significantly more anglers targeting the bugs and fish.

Through the extensive research writing this book, collecting fly patterns, and digging deep into cicada species, I have made new friends and added to the long list of "places to fish before you die." Learning about cicadas in the Deep South, cicadas that border saltwater environments, and cicadas in Mexico, Canada, and locations globally have piqued my interest to ask and, subsequently, find the answers to the question that starts with "I wonder if . . ." This is, after all, *CICADA MADNESS*.

RESOURCES

WEB AND VIRTUAL RESOURCES

Cicada Safari

Cicada Safari is a free app available for iPhone and Android smartphones. This app allows the general public to submit photographs and videos of cicadas where they emerge. Scientists are able to use the location information, photos, and videos to identify species and upload identified broods to a map, allowing the user base to follow the emergence in real time. It is a powerful tool for use by those interested, especially anglers looking to find the bugs that lead them to fish and fishing locations.

www.cicadasafari.org

This website supports the app and has information and links to other research, works, and books regarding the emergence.

www.cicadamania.com

The Cicadamania website is an enormously popular and long running website dedicated to cicadas worldwide. It contains very good resources on identification with thousands of photographs and updated emergence sightings and reports.

www.cicadas.uconn.edu

The University of Connecticut has significant research about cicadas. Many historical records, scientific papers, and a database on emergences are accessible through the site.

www.extension.psu.edu/periodical-cicada

Penn State Extension Office
Article on periodical cicadas by Greg Hoover, edited by Dr. Michael Skvarla

https://naturalhistory.si.edu/education/teaching-resources/life-science/periodical-cicadas

Web page on periodical cicadas from the Smithsonian National Museum of Natural History

www.wiki.bugwood.org
Specialist site that allows for scholar users to update and share knowledge about various insect topics. Wiki-style format enabling search functions. Large amount of cicada data for annual and periodical species.

www.fieldguide.mt.gov
Montana field guide. Contains the cicadas of Montana.

www.idfg.idaho.gov
The Idaho state website for hunting, fishing, and wildlife education. Contains species and locations of cicadas in Idaho. *Platypedia areolata* is the primary species.

www.amazingnature.us
Utah website that contains a list and photographs of insects including the cicadas present in Utah

www.extension.usu.edu
Utah State Extension Office

www.uidaho.edu/extension
Idaho State Extension Office

www.extension.colostate.edu
Colorado State University Extension Office

www.colorado.edu/cumuseum/research-collections/entomology
Colorado Museum of Natural History at Boulder, office of entomology

www.msj.edu/audiences/cicada-media-coverage/index.html
Mount St. Joseph University, Cincinnati, Ohio. Dr. Gene Kritsky's media coverage regarding cicadas and cicada research. Dr. Kritsky is a prominent and world-renowned cicada researcher and founder of the Cicada Safari app.

www.americanwhitewater.org
American Whitewater is a national nonprofit 501(c)(3) river conservation organization whose mission is to protect and restore America's whitewater rivers to enhance opportunities to enjoy them safely. Website has valuable river info including interactive maps.

https://dashboard.waterdata.usgs.gov
The USGS National Water Dashboard is an interactive website with over 13,500 stations nationwide with real-time water flow and gauge information.

BOOKS AND ARTICLES

Alexander, Richard, and Thomas Moore. "The Evolutionary Relationships of 17-Year and 13-Year Cicadas, and Three New Species (Homoptera, Cicadidae, Magicicada)." University of Michigan Museum of Zoology Miscellaneous Publication, 1961, 121. https://www.researchgate.net/publication/30857096_The_evolutionary_relationships_of_17-year_and_13-year_cicadas_and_three_new_species_Homoptera_Cicadidae_Magicicada

Cohen, Pat. *Super Bass Flies: How to Tie and Fish the Most Effective Imitations.* Skyhorse Publishing, 2020.

Cole, J. A., and W. Chatfield-Taylor. "Living Rain Gauges: Cumulative Precipitation Explaining Emergence Schedules of California Protoperiodical Cicadas." *Ecology* 98(10) (2017): 2521–27.

Cooley, John, Gene Kritsky, Marten Edwards, John Zyla, David Marshall, Kathy Hill, Gerry Bunker, Mike Neckermann, Roy Troutman, Jin Yoshimura, and Chris Simon. "Periodical Cicadas (Magicicada spp.): A GIS-Based Map of Broods XIV in 2008 and 'XV' in 2009." *American Entomologist* 57 (2011). 10.1093/ae/57.3.144.

Cooley, John, Gene Kritsky, Marten Edwards, John Zyla, David Marshall, Kathy Hill, Rachel Krauss, and Chris Simon. "The Distribution of Periodical Cicada Brood X in 2004." *American Entomologist* 55 (2009). 10.1093/ae/55.2.106.

Cox, R. T., and C. E. Carlton. "Evidence of Genetic Dominance of the 13-Year Life Cycle in Periodical Cicadas (Homoptera: Cicadidae: Magicicada spp.)." *American Midland Naturalist* 125(1) (1991): 63–74.

Cox, Randel Tom, and Chris E. Carlton. "A Comment on Gene Introgression versus En Masse Cycle Switching in the Evolution of 13-Year and 17-Year Life Cycles in Periodical Cicadas." *Evolution* 57(2) (2003): 428–32. Link: http://www.jstor.org/stable/3094725.

Davis, W. T. "Mississippi Cicadas, with a Key to the Species of the Southeastern United States."*Journal of the New York Entomological Society* 26 (1918): 141–55. Link: https://archive.org/details/biostor-119035/page/n13/mode/2up.

Davis, W. T. "North American Cicadas Belonging to the Genera Platypedia and Melampsalta." *Journal of the New York Entomological Society* 28 (1920): 95–121. Link: https://www.biodiversitylibrary.org/page/8190094#page/119/mode/1up.

Davis, W. T. "Notes on Cicadas from the United States with Descriptions of Several New Species." *Journal of the New York Entomological Society* 24 (1916): 42–65. Link: https://archive.org/details/biostor-119232/page/n21/mode/2up.

Davis, William T. "Cicadas of the Genera Okanagana, Tibicinoides and Okanagodes, with Descriptions of Several New Species." *Journal of the New York Entomological Society* 27 (1919): 179–223. Link: https://www.biodiversitylibrary.org/page/8189764#page/231/mode/1up.

Fujisawa, T., T. Koyama, S. Kakishima, et al. "Triplicate Parallel Life Cycle Divergence Despite Gene Flow in Periodical Cicadas." *Commun Biol* 1(26) (2018). Link: https://doi.org/10.1038/s42003-018-0025-7.

Ito, H., Kakishima, S., Uehara, T. et al. "Evolution of Periodicity in Periodical Cicadas." *Sci Rep* 5, 14094 (2015). Link: https://www.nature.com/articles/srep14094.

Kritsky, Dr. Gene. "Periodical Cicadas: The Brood X Edition." Ohio Biological Survey, Columbus, Ohio, 2021.

Lloyd M., and J. White. "Sympatry of Periodical Cicada Broods and the Hypothetical Four-Year Acceleration." *Evolution: International Journal of Organic Evolution* 30 (Dec. 1, 1976): 786–801.

Marlatt, C. L. "The Periodical Cicada." Bulletin Number 71, U.S. Department of Agriculture Bureau of Entomology, Washington, DC, 1907.

Martin, A., and C. Simon, "Temporal Variation in Insect Life Cycles: Lessons from Periodical Cicadas." *BioScience* 40(5) (1990): 359–67.

Sanborn, A. F., and P. K. Phillips. "Biogeography of the Cicadas (*Hemiptera: Cicadidae*) of North America, North of Mexico." *Diversity* 5 (2013): 166–239. Link: https://doi .org/10.3390/d5020166.

Sanborn, Allen. *Catalogue of the Cicadoidea (Hemiptera: Aucheorrhyncha).* Academic Press, 2014.

Sugden, Dr. John W. "Characteristics of Certain Western Cicadas." University of Utah, Salt Lake City, UT, June 1940. Interesting paper with locations and observations of various cicada species in the western United States. https://www.jstor .org/stable/25004854?seq=1#metadata_info_tab_contents, Link: https://doi .org/10.3390/d5020166.

Takahashi, Rick, and Jerry Hubka. *Modern Terrestrials: Tying and Fishing the World's Most Effective Patterns.* Boiling Springs, PA: Stackpole/Headwater Books, 2014.

Williams, K S, and C Simon. "The Ecology, Behavior and Evolution of Periodical Cicadas." *Annual Review of Entomology* 40(1) (1995), 269–95. Link: https://doi .org/10.1146/annurev.en.40.010195.001413.

VIDEO LINKS

Catching the Hatching, Troutsmith Films
Utah's Green River fly-fishing cicada hatch featuring Colby Crossland.
www.vimeo.com/134164734?embedded=true&source=video_title&owner=34049121

Brood V, Guidefitter Films
Fly fishing and wooden boats on Pennsylvania's Youghiogheny River during the 2016 emergence of Brood V periodical cicadas.
www.youtube.com/watch?v=FYJ6SRLf-Ds

GUIDES, OUTFITTERS, AND FLY SHOPS

Spinnerfall Guide Service
The premier guides on the Green River in
Dutch John, Utah, established in 1986.
PO Box 350
Dutch John, UT 84023
(877) 811-3474
(801) 885-0573
www.spinnerfall.com

Dutch John Resort
Accommodations, boat rentals, and
guide services.
1050 South Blvd.
Dutch John, UT 84023
(435) 848-8000
www.dutchjohnresort.com
frontdesk@dutchjohnresort.com

Flaming Gorge Resort
Accommodations, guide fishing,
fly shop, groceries, restaurant, and
accommodations.
1100 E. Flaming Gorge
Dutch John, UT 84023
(435) 889-3773
www.flaminggorgeresort.com

Red Canyon Lodge
Mountain lodging, dining, non-fishing
activities, guided hunting, fishing, and
outdoor adventures in the Flaming Gorge
National Recreation Area.
2450 W. Red Canyon Lodge
Dutch John, UT 84023
(435) 889-3759
www.redcanyonlodge.com

Western Rivers Flyfisher
Well-stocked Salt Lake City Fly shop
with a knowledgeable staff.
1071 E. 900 S.
Salt Lake City, UT 84105
(801) 521-6424
www.westernriversflyfishing.com

Western Rivers Fly-fishing Guides
Guided float and walk-wade trips, shuttle
service, lodging, and fly shop.
555 S. Center St.
Dutch John, UT 84023
(435) 790-6465
www.wrfguides.com

Trout Creek Flies
Guide service, fly shop, lodging, groceries, RV park, and shuttle service.
1155 Little Hole Rd.
Dutch John, UT 84023
(435) 885-3355
www.troutcreekflies.com

Dry Fly Utah
Guide service for Nick Jackson on the
Green River, Utah.
(801) 706-7836
www.dryflyutah.com

Old Moe Guide Service
Guide service and limited lodging in
Dutch John, Utah, on the Green River.
PO Box 293
Dutch John, UT 84023
(435) 885-3342
www.oldmoeguideservice.com

TCO Fly Shop
Pennsylvania's premier fly shop with four
locations. Well-stocked fly-tying section
and local fly selections. Well-maintained
stream reports on all the major Pennsylvania fly-fishing creeks and rivers.
www.tcoflyfishing.com

TCO State College
2030 E. College Ave.
State College, PA 16801
(814) 689-3654

TCO Bryn Mawr
834 W. Lancaster Ave.
Bryn Mawr, PA 19010
(610) 527-3388

TCO Boiling Springs
2 E. 1st St.
Boiling Springs, PA 17007
(717) 609-0169

TCO Reading
2229 Penn Ave.
West Lawn, PA 19609
(610) 678-1899

Eastern Trophies
Guide service on the Potomac, North
Branch Potomac, and Shenandoah Rivers
for trophy smallmouth. Exclusive supplier
of Chuck Kraft–style flies and materials.
(571) 213-2570
www.easterntrophies.com

Marble Canyon Outfitters
Guide service on Arizona's Colorado
River at Lees Ferry.
PO Box 272
Fredonia, AZ 86022
(800) 533-7339
www.leesferryflyfishing.com

Marble Canyon Lodge
Accommodations, restaurant, air strip,
fuel, and amenities.
Marble Canyon Lodge
Marble Canyon, AZ 86036
(928) 355-2225
www.marblecanyoncompany.com

Lees Ferry Anglers
Fly shop, guide service, boat rentals, and
Cliff Dwellers Lodge and Restaurant at
Lees Ferry on the Colorado River.
HC 67, Box 30
Marble Canyon, AZ 86036
(800) 962-9755
(928) 355-2261
www.leesferry.com

Laurel Highlands Guide Service
Guided fishing trips on the Youghiogheny River in Pennsylvania. Float and
wade-fishing for trout, smallmouth bass,
musky, and carp.
Rob Walters
(412) 715-8461
www.laurelhighlandsguideservices.com

Contented Angler
A genuine fly shop with a well-
stocked fly-tying material selection and
custom-tied flies.
147 Jefferson Dr.
Lower Burrell, PA 15068
(724) 337-0437
www.content-angler.com

Savage River Outfitters
Fly shop and lodging located on the banks
of the blue-ribbon Savage River in north-
western Maryland. Close proximity to the
North Branch of the Potomac River, Deep
Creek, and the Savage River State Forest.
2721 Savage River Rd.
Swanton, MD 21561
(703) 517-1040
(301) 707-1934
www.savageriveroutfitters.com

International Angler
Pittsburgh, Pennsylvania's premier fly
shop and guide service.
5275 Steubenville Pike
Pittsburgh, PA 15205
(412) 788-8088
www.internationalangler.com

Schultz Outfitters
Southeast Michigan guide service.
(734) 544-1761
www.schultzoutfitters.com

Mad River Outfitters
South-central Ohio fly shop
and guide service.
833 Bethel Rd.
Columbus, OH 43214
(624) 451-0363
www.madriveroutfitters.com

The Backpackers Shop
Fly shop, outdoor gear, and guided trips.
5128 Colorado Ave.
Sheffield, OH 44054
(440) 934-5345
www.backpackersshop.com

Mossy Creek Fly Fishing
Fly shop and guide service on Mossy
Creek offering float trips on the Shenandoah and James Rivers.
480 E. Market St.
Harrisonburg, VA 22801
(540) 434-2444
www.mossycreekflyfishing.com

Knee Deep Fly Fishing LLC
Micah Dammeyer offers guiding and
instruction in the Washington, DC, and
capital region.
(202) 681-8765
www.kneedeepff.com

Pro River Outfitters
Guided fly fishing on West Virginia's
upper and lower New River and Gauley
River. Fully equipped with raft, jet boat,
and drift boat options. Bobby Bower is a
West Virginia native with over 30 years'
experience guiding these rivers.
3224 Court St.
Fayetteville, WV 25840
(304) 575-5252
www.profishwv.com

Front Range Anglers
Colorado fly shop and guide service
located in Boulder, Colorado.
2344 Pearl St.
Boulder, CO 80302
(877) 935-2975
www.frontrangeanglers.com

Kirk's Fly Shop
Fly shop and guide service located in
Estes Park, Colorado; source for outdoor gear and trips into Rocky Mountain
National Park and surrounding areas.
230 E. Elkhorn Ave.
Estes Park, CO 80517
(970) 577-0790
(877) 669-1859
www.kirksflyshop.com

FLIES AND FLY-TYING MATERIALS

J. Stockard Flyfishing
www.jsflyfishing.com

Rainy's Flies
www.rainysflies.com

Fly Fish Food
www.flyfishfood.com

Montana Fly Company
www.mfcfishing.com

Umpqua Feather Merchants
www.umpqua.com

Hareline
www.hairline.com

Blane Chocklett
Blane Chocklett needs no introduction in the fishing world. Blane is a highly innova-tive fly tier, guide, and author with a lifetime of experience trying new things on the water. He is influential not only in his fly designs, but in his involvement with fly rod design with Temple Fork Outfitters, and a long history of conventional fishing around the Southeast. Blane guides his home waters around Roanoke, Virginia.
www.blanechocklett.com

Flymen Fishing Company
Flymen Fishing Company, based in South Carolina, manufactures and distributes many innovative fly-tying products and patterns, and is a primary distributor of Blane Chocklett's signature flies as well as several innovative materials.
www.flymenfishingcompany.com

Andrew Grillos
Andrew Grillos is a legendary guide and fly tier currently residing in Bozeman, Mon-tana. Andrew's experiences are vast, from commercial fly tying in his late teen years to his time spent guiding in Colorado, Montana, Washington, Argentina, Alaska, and Chile. Andrew's flies often blend traditional materials with modern materials, and his dry flies almost always incorporate a creative use of foam. He is as creative with the naming of his patterns as the flies themselves: Hippie Stomper, '64 Impala, Dancin' Ricky, and Grillo's Great Carpholio, to name a few. Andrew and I became friends through our love for fly fishing as well as a mutual connection to our misspent youths as skateboarders and punk rock listeners.
www.andrewgrillosflyfishing.com

Pat Cohen's Superfly
Pat Cohen's website offers his signature patterns and materials. Pat is a tattoo artist, smallmouth bass enthusiast, illustrator, and author from upstate New York. Pat's deer hair cicadas are works of functional art, and he was kind enough to provide his flies for use in this book.
www.rusuperfly.com

FrankenFly
FrankenFly is an online resource of all things fly tying, with innovative patterns and a blog and forum with excellent photography. Search "Cicada" for multiple patterns.
www.frankenfly.com

Charlie's Fly Box
Charlie Craven's website for fly patterns, tying materials, and fly-fishing gear, including online tying videos and tutorials.
www.charliesflybox.com

Feather-Craft
St. Louis–based fly shop, family owned since 1955 by Ed Story, now run by his son Bob. Online fly-fishing store with a well-stocked fly-tying section with hard-to-find items.
8307 Manchester Rd.
St. Louis, MO 63144
(800) 659-1707
www.feather-craft.com

Envision Fly Works
Steve Yewchuck's Instagram page containing his innovative and functional fly patterns.
@envisionflyworks

Panther Branch Bugs
Brandon Baile's Instagram page containing his expertly crafted flies.
@pantherbranchbugs

ORGANIZATIONS

Little Juniata River Association (LJRA)
LJRA's mission is "to monitor and improve the Little Juniata River and its tributaries as coldwater resources."
www.littlejuniata.net

Trout Unlimited
"We bring diverse interests to care for and recover rivers and streams, so our children can experience the joy of wild and native trout and salmon."
www.tu.org

INDEX

James, Wade, x
Juniata River, 73

Knee Deep Fly Fishing, 108
Kraft, Chuck, 105. *See also* Chuck
    Kraft Excalibur
Kritsky, Gene, 5, 12, 14, 37
Krueger, Chris, 119

lake fishing
    for carp, 43–44, 131–32
    cicada gatherings, 137
    flooded timber and, 135
    points of land projecting out, 134–35
    protected coves, 133–34
    shoreline game, 132–33, 135
    steep banks, 136
larval form cicadas, 22, 25, 30, 38
Laurel Highlands Guide Service, 52,
    64, 114, 138
Laurel Hill Creek, 65
Lee, Dron, Fused Body Cicada X, 107
Lees Ferry, xii, 29, 31–32, 79
life cycle of periodical cicadas, 9, 10,
    12–13, 22–23
line hand management, 129
Little Juniata River, 73–75
Logan Valley, 73
Lovejoy, Brad, cicada patterns, 117–18
Ludwig, Steve, x, 35, 46, 62, 113–14

Magicicada genus. *See* periodical cicadas
Marinaro, Vince, 2
markers, permanent, 84
Marlatt, Charles Lester, 5
Mason, Paul, 112
mating calls, 19–22, 28–29, 31
Maxima Chameleon, 142
McCoy-Linn Dam, 72
Meadow Run, 65
mondo cicada, 24, 31, 69, 77, 78, 118
Monongahela River, 62
Moodah Poodah pattern, 112
Mormon Crickets, 2, 77, 78
mountain cicadas, 38, 94–96, 119
Mount St. Joseph University, Center for IT
    Engagement, 37
Mowgli, Dan, 37
Mueller, Geoff, 20

Neotibicen species, 16, 17, 21, 27, 70, 106
night fishing, 53
Ninja Cicada pattern, 113
nymphal cicadas, 12–13, 17

Ohiopyle, Pennsylvania, 63–65
Ohiopyle Falls, 65
Okanagana bella, 38
Okanagana bella Davis cicadas, 99
Okanagana bella varieties, 119
Okanagana magnifica cicada, 27, 48, 77, 119
Okanagana species, 23–24

Panther Branch Bugs Annual Cicada
    pattern, 120
Panther Branch Bugs Spent Cicada
    pattern, 121
Penns Cave, 73
Penns Creek, 72–73
Penn State University, Science Department, 36
Pennsylvania Department of Parks, 52
Pennsylvania Fish and Boat
    Commission, 63, 64
Pennsylvania Game Commission, 12
periodical cicadas
    Brood classification for, 5–6
    brood distribution, 7–8
    brood distribution map, 6
    coloration, 5
    as diurnal, 18–19
    emergence, ix–x
    emergence process, 14–19
    evolution of, 9
    flying behavior, 20–21
    global distribution, 30
    identifying adult forms, 5
    imitations. *See* cicada patterns
    interbreeding of broods, 12
    intervals for, 4
    life cycle, 9, 10, 12–13, 22–23
    mating activity, 21–22
    mating calls, 19–22
    metamorphosis to flying adult, 18
    molting process, 13
    nymphal stages, 12–13
    predators of, 11–12, 25
    research for. *See* information gathering
    seasonal change detection of, 14
    straggler emergences, 14
    temperature affects on, 18–19
    threats to, 30

ABOUT THE AUTHOR

FOR THE LAST 20 YEARS, **DAVE ZIELINSKI** HAS BEEN TRACKING DOWN periodical cicada emergences in an effort to figure out their mystery and the fish that hunt and devour them. Dave's book *Cicada Madness: Timing, Fishing Techniques, and Patterns for Cracking the Code of Epic Cicada Emergences* is the culmination of his experiences and is currently the only dedicated resource for fly fishing and cicadas.

Dave resides in rural western Pennsylvania with his wife, three daughters, and two German shorthaired pointers where he spends his spring and summer chasing fish and chasing birds over dogs in the fall. He also is also the owner and operator of Down Home Boat Works, where he designs and builds custom wooden drift boats for fly fishing and river running.

The author with a rainbow trout caught on a cicada pattern. WADE JAMES